Property Management in Real Estate Investment Decision-Making

Lexington Books Special Series in Real Estate and Urban Land Economics

William N. Kinnard, Jr., Editor

James H. Boykin, *Financing Real Estate*
D. Barlow Burke, *American Conveyancing Patterns*
James R. Cooper and Karl Guntermann, *Real Estate and Urban Land Analysis*
Gene Dilmore, *Real-Estate Counseling*
Leo Grebler and Frank G. Mittlebach, *The Inflation of House Prices*
Gaylon E. Greer, *The Real-Estate Investment Decision*
Austin J. Jaffe, *Property Management in Real Estate Investment Decision-Making*
Irvin E. Johnson, *The Instant Mortgage-Equity Technique*
Irvin E. Johnson, *Selling Real Estate by Mortgage-Equity Analysis*
William N. Kinnard, Jr., *Income Property Valuation*
William N. Kinnard, Jr., *Principles and Techniques of Real Property Appraising*
William N. Kinnard, Jr., and Stephen D. Messner, *Effective Business Relocation*
Robert A. Sigafoos, *Corporate Real Estate Development*
Leonard P. Vidger, *Borrowing and Lending on Real Estate*

Property Management in Real Estate Investment Decision-Making

Austin J. Jaffe
University of Oregon

Lexington Books
D.C. Heath and Company
Lexington, Massachusetts
Toronto

Library of Congress Cataloging in Publication Data

Jaffe, Austin J.
Property management in real estate investment decision-making.

Bibliography: p.
Includes index.
1. Real estate investment—Mathematical models.
I. Title.
HD1375.J33 658.1'5242 78-19911
ISBN 0-669-02453-8

Published simultaneously in Canada.

Printed in the United States of America.

International Standard Book Number: 0-669-02453-8

Library of Congress Catalog Card Number: 78-19911

To my parents,
Shirley and Aaron Jaffe

Contents

List of Figures and Tables

Figures

Tables

Acknowledgments

The author wishes to thank the many persons who directly or indirectly assisted in the preparation of this text. A debt of thanks goes to the faculty and staff of the Department of Finance at the University of Illinois at Urbana-Champaign. Assistance and support significantly aided in the preparation of this study from the Bureau of Business Research and the Department of Finance of the College of Business Administration at the University of Oregon. Valuable comments and suggestions were offered by Professor C.F. Sirmans, Jr., of the University of Georgia and Professor Jerome Dasso of the University of Oregon.

Exceptional manuscript preparation was provided by Carolyn B. Sherrell. The Graphic Arts Service of the University of Oregon assisted with visual aids. However, despite this valuable assistance, the responsibility for any errors or omissions in the text rests solely with the author.

Introduction

The modeling of real estate investment has grown with the development of the digital computer in the late 1960s and early 1970s. This does not suggest that investment analysis began when computer programmers first appeared on the scene. On the contrary, investment analysis was born as the first investment decision was made. While the method of analysis was no doubt crude, the basis of the decision was made by some, albeit obscure, manner. This enabled selection of one alternative over another. With this development, decision theory and real estate investment analysis had their beginnings.

Ricks observed that the state of the art in 1964 in real estate investment analysis lacked a body of literature and thus a theory of investment.[1] He cited that failure to quantify many of the important considerations such as objectives, risks, and decision rules led analysts to base their decisions on little analysis and much descriptive dialogue.

While development occurred at a rapid pace in the following few years, the theory of real estate investment tended to lag behind quantitative and theoretical advancements in related disciplines. Seldin and Swesnik's text did little to quantify the "investment strategy." They did, however, promise good fortune to investors presumably since land is "where the big money can be made,"[2] and "ownership of real estate is prestigious."[3] Their claims were justified by institutional analysis typical in the following statements: "The risks are low [in investing in garden apartments] because well designed and well located properties rent well. . ."[4] or, "High rise apartments are more desirable and more costly than garden apartments."[5]

Another comparable investment text was written by Beaton.[6] While it failed to contain any investment models or theory, it provided readers with institutional background on depreciation, taxation, ownership forms, and alternative real estate investment categories, as most writers had previously done. Recently, a revised edition by Beaton and Robertson attempted to correct the lack of theoretical modeling of the initial edition, but retained the same cookbook format.[7]

The texts of Ratcliff[8] and Wendt and Cerf[9] seem to be exceptions to this criticism. Ratcliff's book, although written in 1961, provided the foundations of theoretical real estate analysis which eventually blossomed in the mid-1970s. Ratcliff's regard for an economist's appreciation and understanding of the urban economic environment paved the way for later investment modeling and implicit consideration of location. Although far from modeling the investment process, Ratcliff suggested the connection between valuation and the analyst's goal is time-related since "the objective of the analyst is to predict the most probable future productivity."[10]

Wendt and Cert's monumental text set the quantitative foundation for modern real estate investment analysis.[11] Its major contribution was to provide a framework of theoretical analysis of the rate of return calculation inherent in the investment decision. The reemergence of the after-tax-cash-flow-to-equity model, after having been introduced in an earlier paper,[12] supplied the discipline with an investment model and decision-making framework which has been the building block for more sophisticated analysis ever since.

Cooper's text paid tribute to this development by emphasizing that "it is generally recognized that the after-tax return on equity is the most significant measure of real estate investment returns."[13] Cooper surveyed the development based upon traditional analysis and developments in finance.

Recent texts by Maisel and Roulac[14] and Messner, Schreiber, and Lyon[15] show some of the theoretical advancements found in earlier seminal literature. Both texts adopt a decision-making approach, using a modified quantitative approach to the study of investment analysis for real estate projects. The problem is not whether or not real estate investment modeling has been introduced, but rather how well it is understood.

As evidenced by its title, *Real Estate Investment Analysis and Taxation,* Wendt and Cerf's book emphasized tax considerations as an integral part of the investment process. This emphasis turned into an assumption on the part of many writers since its publication. As analysis become more sophisticated, writers and analysts looked toward other considerations as well. Variables such as depreciation, tax shelter benefits, depreciable lives of property, mortgage terms, mortgage interest rates, loan to value ratios, reversion growth rates, or holding periods have been analyzed at various lengths by many authors. Most of these variables have been assumed to command a paramount position in their impact on investment decisions. For a few, such as depreciation and tax shelter benefits, together with marginal and capital gains tax rates, analysis has been given primary attention nearly universally in the world of real estate investment analysis.

Purposé of the Study

The primary purpose of this study is to examine the theoretical relationships between important variables found in the equity valuation real estate investment model. This research is an examination of real estate investment analysis to determine the relative importance of certain variables over others. This result can be measured by observing their impact on value and rate of return. The thesis of this study is that certain variables, which were thought to be very influential on rate of return and value, are not as influential as traditionally thought. Similarly, other variables, such as property management, are more influential than the traditional literature has held.

This study is made up of five steps:

1. Examining the literature of computerized real estate modeling to demonstrate the historical direction and methodologies of decision-making tools. Special attention is devoted to presumptions of importance of input variables in the decision-making process. A review of the initial case studies provides the historical perspective.
2. Developing the mathematical analysis of sensitivity analysis, enabling the examination of the impact that chosen input variables have on real estate investment analysis.
3. Developing the computerization of the sensitivity functions for changes in value and rate of return as a result of changes in many input variables.
4. Presenting empirical data and discussing the relevance of various sensitivity functions, given the distribution of empirical observations.
5. Testing the Walters' "importance of property management" hypothesis[16] and therefore redirecting interest to those variables important in the decision-making process. The importance of property management hypothesis suggests that the variables under the control of the property manager may be the most important variables in the investment valuation process.

Traditionally, variables such as gross income and operating expenses tended to be overlooked as important investment decision variables. Obviously, unfavorable shifts in either of these variables would suggest concern for the investor, but as implied earlier, most of the analysis centered around taxation or depreciation considerations. To date, a complete analysis has been neglected on the part of real estate writers. Consequently, this analysis hopes to make a contribution to the real estate investment and management literature by redirecting interest to those variables that are most important or significant, in terms of their impact on value or rate of return. However, initially, those variables must be determined. Thus this research seeks to directly test Walters' importance of property management hypothesis.

In addition, this work hopes to clarify and specify the importance of sound modeling, simulation, and decision theory which seems to have been overlooked in much of the real estate literature. Since "model-building is the essence of the operations research approach,"[17] the mastering of basic operations research methodology is imperative.

The importance of these problems should be apparent. If the literature of real estate investment modeling has neglected certain variables which are important in favor of others, it seems necessary to redirect attention to those variables which are important in the decision-making process. This research demonstrates the importance of these results to investors, lenders, and analysts.

By developing the mathematical analysis of the technique of sensitivity analysis and by computerizing the model, this research presents a framework to solve the problem posed above. The introduction of empirical data analysis should satisfy possible objections based upon theories of institutional input evaluation and the presumed lack of distribution for certain input parameters.

Since modeling and simulation studies are concepts and techniques adapted from other academic areas, real estate model building and theories of simulation must conform to developments and findings in those areas. Modeling theory has been largely neglected in real estate writings. The failure to link these areas is bridged in this work.

Finally and most importantly, we hope to be able to better understand the role of management in investment decisions. If property management is "the single most important area of concern in real estate investment analysis,"[18] as Walters suggests, a new direction may be necessary in analyzing real estate investment projects. The link between successful investment decisions and effective management has often been assumed to be a weak one. This work demonstrates the danger of such a proposition.

Organization of the Study

Chapter 1 presents a review of the literature of computerized real estate modeling. Traditional methodology, criteria, goals, and decision rules are discussed. A comparison between deterministic and probabilistic real estate models is presented, with special emphasis placed on treatment of risk, uncertainty, and modeling. A review is also made of investment analysis in relation to developments such as Ellwood capitalization and traditional appraisal theory, decision theory applications, portfolio theory with real estate holdings, and challenges to the traditional discounted cash flow approach. A discussion also relates the current emphasis placed on certain variables important in the examination of the thesis of this study.

Chapter 2 reviews the development of decision analysis in operations research and management science as it relates to the modeling of capital investment. In addition to reviewing the theory of models and the modeling process, it also highlights the theory and use of sensitivity analysis as a technique in decision analysis in various areas in economics and business research. Emphasis is placed on the assumptions, limitations, and problems of previous work. The development of this chapter may well help to link decision analysis and the theory of models with capital investment in real property.

A review of various empirical discounted cash flow studies that have appeared in real estate literature is presented in chapter 3. Initially, a survey is made of those rate of return studies found in the real estate area. A few attempts have also explicitly compared investment in real property to alternative investments such as common stock. In addition, a number of authors have either advocated sensitivity studies or conducted partial studies, examining those variables thought to be influential. This survey essentially reviews the rate of return studies made previously in the literature. In particular, it compares those studies that have incorporated sensitivity analysis into decision-making models.

Chapter 4 presents the investment model to be used in the analysis. The mathematical relationships are specified and the results given and summarized. In addition, the computerization of the model yields detailed and specific results for the parameters tested, based upon the assumptions employed.

In chapter 5 the sensitivity functions derived in chapter 4 are examined in light of empirical data. The data show where the theoretical functional relationships are meaningful, given the investment climate and conditions in the recent past. For certain variables the range of distributions of actual values is considerably greater than for others. Since theoretical sensitivities are meaningful only when the observed range of values is somewhat dispersed, this part is considered crucial to the identification of sensitive variables. If one variable had a very significant theoretical sensitivity function but its range by observation was very narrow, the real-world implication of the theoretical result would have little meaning. In fact, it could be very misleading.

Chapter 6 presents a discussion of the results of the study and implications of its findings. Principally, the results indicate the extent to which Walters' hypothesis can be upheld theoretically as well as empirically. In the end, it discusses the necessity of redirection of analysis, given the results.

Chapter 7 concludes the study, suggests limitations of the sensitivity analysis approach, and presents suggestions for further research. Since the policy recommendations and implications of this study are of major interest, these are discussed as well.

Notes

1. R. Bruce Ricks, *Recent Trends in Institutional Real Estate Investment,* Research Report, no. 23 (Berkeley, Calif.: University of California, Center for Real Estate and Urban Economics, Institute of Urban and Regional Development, 1964), p. 1.

2. Maury Seldin and Richard H. Swesnik, *Real Estate Investment Strategy* (New York: Wiley-Interscience, 1970), p. 137.

3. Ibid., p. 4.

4. Ibid., p. 168.

5. Ibid., p. 177.

6. William R. Beaton, *Real Estate Investment* (Englewood Cliffs, N.J.: Prentice-Hall, 1971).

7. William R. Beaton and Terry Robertson, *Real Estate Investment,* 2d ed. (Englewood Cliffs, N.J.: Prentice-Hall, 1977).

8. Richard U. Ratcliff, *Real Estate Analysis* (New York: McGraw-Hill Book Co., 1961).

9. Paul F. Wendt and Alan R. Cerf, *Real Estate Investment Analysis and Taxation* (New York: McGraw-Hill Book Co., 1969).

10. Ratcliff, *Real Estate Analysis,* p. 115.

11. Wendt and Cerf, *Real Estate Investment.*

12. Paul F. Wendt and Sui N. Wong, "Investment Performance: Common Stocks Versus Apartment Houses," *Journal of Finance* 20 (December 1965): 633-646.

13. James R. Cooper, *Real Estate Investment Analysis* (Lexington, Mass.: Lexington Books, D.C. Heath and Co., 1974), p. 8.

14. Sherman J. Maisel and Stephen E. Roulac, *Real Estate Investment and Finance* (New York: McGraw-Hill Book Co., 1976).

15. Stephen D. Messner, Irving Schreiber, and Victor L. Lyon, *Marketing Investment Real Estate* (Chicago: Realtors National Marketing Institute of the National Association of Realtors, 1975).

16. David W. Walters, "Just How Important Is Property Management?" *Journal of Property Management* 38 (July/August 1973): 164–168.

17. Harvey M. Wagner, *Principles of Management Science,* 2d ed. (Englewood Cliffs, N.J.: Prentice-Hall, 1975), p. 7.

18. Walters, "Property Management."

1 History and Emphasis of Real Estate Investment Modeling

Goals and Motivations of Real Estate Investors

Real estate investment attracts many investors for many reasons. However. investor goals are often dissimiliar from the investment opportunities available. This section presents background dealing with many of the concerns and elements of real estate investment analysis.

It also discusses the relationship that many of the factors in the real estate investment process have to return and value. Many writers have looked at various factors and their impacts on value. In addition, many writers have urged careful analysis of certain variables in the valuation process of real estate projects. The fact that a lack of agreement exists regarding which variables are crucial warrants this review. In particular, the literature of taxation, credit analysis, and property management is extensively reviewed.

Factors Affecting Real Estate Values

The identification and magnitude of the relevant factors that affect real estate values are very directly related to the work of an appraiser. The traditional three-approach appraisal methodology attempts to identify the relevant considerations in each approach. The dogma of the three separate approaches, while stemming from three separate strains of economic thought, is essentially linked to one central concept: estimation of market valuation. The former criticism of the traditional methodology has become increasingly well known and accepted.[1]

The classic list of factors affecting returns on real estate can be found in Babcock.[2] Covering nearly all possible relevant items, the classification centers upon such factors as location, stability of returns, risk of future alterations, and the functional aspects of the property. In one sense, nearly all of the subsequent work in this area has examined the influence on return of one or more of the variables Babcock had categorized.

Much work has been done using hedonic price equations on the determinants of land values.[3] Other writers have looked at the impact of external influences, such as pollution,[4] zoning, [5] or taxation.[6] Most of this work has not been considered as a part of real estate investment analysis but rather as market analysis, with particular interest in the effect of the particular factor.

Within the classic three-approach appraisal methodology, the income approach is most closely related to investment analysis. Regardless of the degree of sophistication used regarding the calculation of return and capitalization, appraisers tend to consider two factors as most important: the income stream and the capitalization rate. The precise definition and appropriate use of each of these depends upon the appraiser; but under the cost approach, changes in either of these variables would result in significant impact in the appraiser's estimate of value.

Maisel and Roulac recently concluded that "real estate values are affected by changes in population, location, incomes, and prices."[7] However, they also suggest that the "primary factors which must be examined to make good forecasts and proper [valuation] decisions" are projections of income and costs, management, financial arrangements, and governmental influences.[8] Thus, this general framework cannot enable us to identify specifically the important factors and determinants of value.

But Ricks suggested that the value of real estate may be a definitional problem, depending upon the value to be estimated. He alerted analysts to the problem of investment forecasting rather than market valuation.[9] Therefore, the relationship between market valuation and investment analysis is important.

Appraisal versus Investment Analysis

Many writers have suggested a close relationship between investment decision-making and market appraisal. Most simply, this can be viewed as the difference in the function of the work. Ricks suggested that calculating the expected rate of return in investment analysis was the activity similar to estimating fair market value for the appraiser.[10] In addition, he stated that one possible explanation for the lack of theory in 1964 was "a concentration on establishing fair market value."[11]

Since traditional appraisal theory values property before taxes, valuation or rate of return calculations are not taken into account. Ricks also observed that the pre-1960s valuation doctrine made appraisal methods inadequate for investment analysis.[12] He concluded by endorsing an after-tax cash flow formula to calculate yield for the investor. Other models appeared in the next few years.

In "Investment Analysis in Appraising," Smith linked the two areas by illustrating that expenses treated by individual investors could be included in the appraisal process.[13] He viewed investment analysis as a special case of appraisal methodology; assuming appraisers could be estimating what Ratcliff called V_P (most probably selling price), then investment analysis could be a valid valuation process.

In their critique of the traditional appraisal doctrine, Smith and Racster defined the justified investment price (JIP) as an individualized value that the investor could afford to pay after specifying a rate of return on his investment.[14] They concluded by advocating the inclusion of JIP with an estimate of market value in the appraisal process.[15]

Graaskamp argued that the use of an investment model could be used as an appraisal technique. He also suggested that computerized investment models could be extensively used to predict market value, although their intentions were directed to particular users.[16] Kinnard argued in his investment property appraisal text that the calculation of investment value was also an important consideration for the appraiser of investment property. He emphasized that clear definitions are necessary for investment value, market value, and other related concepts.

However, Hanford adopted the minority view. He emphasized that discounted cash flow analysis was not an appraisal method and was not very useful for appraisers. His article demonstrated a DCF model, typically used in real estate investment analysis, and suggested that its use for appraisal is limited to "buy-sell decision-making."[17] He also suggested considerable use of the DCF model by appraisers may be a long way away.

Attractiveness of Real Estate as an Investment

Generations of investors have no doubt been fascinated by returns available from investment in real property. Many writers have expressed possible reasons for such interest, some of which have not always been economically sound.

In "The Psychology of Real Estate Investments," Peatman suggested that investment in real estate could be explained for one or more of three reasons: security, yield, or speculation.[18] While these seem broad and overly general criteria, many later writers failed to suggest better reasons. Actually, many writers merely suggested important variables based upon prior beliefs and personal factors.

Another point of view was expressed by Bedford. He suggested five major reasons why real estate "stands on one side, as all other forms of security stands [*sic*] on the other side."[19] These include production of rental income, returns at a fixed rate of interest, security in home ownership, locational advantages for a future business, and yield from agricultural land. He also remarked that "it goes without argument that the basic values of all forms of securities and investments are fundamentally dependent on the basic value of real estate."[20] Furthermore, he noted that most real estate that produced income for the past 100 years was still producing, and, in most cases, "has increased its productivity many times over."[21]

He concluded with this paragraph: "Real estate stands alone, above all other securities, as the safest, soundest investment in the world. It has the smallest percentage of risk. Regardless of what may happen, real estate will always have value.[22]

While other writers in the 1940s may have disagreed with many of these statements, the article appeared in *The Appraisal Journal,* the official publication of the American Institute of Real Estate Appraisers. Furthermore, it illustrates the lack of development in the area of real estate investment analysis.

By 1960, the state of the art had advanced, but only slightly, as evidenced by Landauer's "Real Estate as an Investment."[23] The thesis of his paper was that "real property affords the best investment a man can make because of the basic uniqueness of real estate."[24] Many of the myths commonly propagated today appear to have begun about this time. He argued that the fundamental reason real property was the best investment was because land was limited in quantity, that is, scarce. In addition, since population was constantly increasing, this always implied a greater demand for land. In the case of corporate stocks or bonds, new issues would increase the supply, much to the regret of earlier holders of the securities, whereas holders of land cannot suffer this anomaly.[25] Landauer's article is particularly important because it identified as the vital keys to favorable investment" two considerations which are still extensively examined today: depreciation and capital gains potential. In addition, he cited other reasons for investment such as real estate's inherent ability as an inflation hedge, an implicit higher rate of return, greater leverage advantages, better tax benefits, advantages of owning a real asset, the availability of corporate forms, and exchange programs to defer tax liability.[26] As is well known to all students of real estate economics, none of these advantages is available without risk or cost. In fact, many may not be available to real estate at all.

One of the leading textbooks in real estate investment and appraisal valuation was written by Kahn, Case, and Schimmel.[27] The text consisted entirely of institutional treatment of real estate investment decisions. It was marred by a lack of decision-making criteria, and the level of analysis rested upon the intuition of the investor as to the attractiveness of certain properties and to the social policy of the times.

A study by Grebler, published in 1955, was the first of many empirical studies which would appear considerably later in the literature.[28] His study assumed investment in real estate to be a long-term proposition since most investors would be interested in "modest but secure income."[29] In fact, property data were used only if the holding period was at least twenty years, which when reduced further, amounted to 312 cases, including 581 properties.[30] While the study has some conceptual problems about rate of return measurement and data sources, he concluded that investment in real estate "refers to investment in urban income problems held over a long period of time, usually several decades."[31]

A survey of literature by Case was chiefly concerned with available rates of return from real estate projects.[32] However, the lack of a sound theoretical base for measuring returns led him to rely upon two ratios as measures of rates of return: operating expense ratio and net operating income to cost ratio.[33] The implication was that investors will be concerned about these ratios (or changes in these ratios) since they are appropriate measures of return. Case suggested that changes in operating expenses as a percentage of gross income (and thus net operating income as a percentage of cost) are crucial concerns for investors.

Recent writers have tended to suggest taxation as a major consideration for investors. Hayes and Harlan stated that the "tax shield on real estate was the essence of the profit potential."[34] Smith found that smaller investors were primarily interested in tax shelter, and that cash flows or long-term yield seemed to be of little importance to those investors.[35] He also suggested that the final investment value should be stated in terms of tax shelter and equity growth as well as net income.[36]

A recent paper by Downs and Lachman suggests four main advantages of a real estate investment: tax shelter potential, long-term capital gains, levered high rates of return, and the offer of psychological returns.[37] They also warn of the disadvantages inherent in real estate investment such as illiquidity, concern over management, necessity of expert advice, modest overall rates of return on total capital, riskiness, and lack of volatile income streams.[38]

With the development of investment models, the assumption that has received primary emphasis is the goal of maximizing the owner's financial position. This is commonly accomplished by maximizing the valuation of the investor's project or similarly by maximizing the rate of return (yield) on available projects, given some acceptable reinvestment rate assumption. The modeling process then has removed the ambiguity of the investment process by transforming relevant considerations into a symbolic form. By maximizing the valuation model, the investor has maximized his financial position and, thus by assumption, achieved his stated objective.

Surveys of Reasons for Real Estate Investment

In 1971 the U.S. Department of Housing and Urban Development (HUD) conducted an extensive survey of 137 investors from 434 properties in six large urban cities.[39] The survey asked participants to rank seven criteria according to how important each item was to the investor. The results indicated that cash flow and tax shelter were regarded as more important by most investors. Less important factors included liquidity, low risk, capital appreciation, leverage, and fees from packaging. In addition, only 49 percent of the active investors in the study considered alternative investments other than their current real estate holdings. In contrast, 82 percent of the passive investors considered other investments and most did not consider only real estate ventures.[40]

A study by Davis indicated 377 reasons for investment in real estate.[41] The most frequent response was capital gains, followed by tax shelter, forced saving, and inflation protection (see table 1-1). The least important was the advice of the broker. For two-to-four unit residences, tax shelter is the reason reported as most important.

A recent study by Wiley indicated that investors emphasized return on equity as a measure of performance. The study also indicated that investors placed a primary concern on cash flow to equity in the investment decision.[42] While the thrust of this survey was centered more on techniques and models, the author concluded that as a result of the use of after-tax analysis, "there is widespread recognition in the investment community of the important influence of tax factors on the value of investment properties."[43]

The Importance of Taxation to Real Estate

A text prepared for the National Institute of Farm and Land Brokers argued that the link between real estate returns and tax planning cannot be overlooked. This text suggested many tax advantages for well-planned investments and promised greater capital growth as a result.[44] This basic position has also been adopted by a number of authors, including Cerf,[45] Wendt and Cerf,[46] Higgins[47] Wendt,[48] Boyce and Higgins,[49] HUD,[50] Smith, Tschappat, and Racster,[51] Wyndelts,[52] and McMahan.[53]

Cerf's book emphasized tax considerations for the real estate analyst. In particular, he pointed out that the rate of return calculation was sensitive to tax planning. The investor can make use of his funds more effectively by evaluating projects on an after-tax basis. But he also warned that tax planning is not a panacea. If the analyst were to devote all of his time and effort to tax planning and avoidance, the investor could "give too much weight to the tax factors."[54]

Wendt and Cerf devoted much of the impetus of their text to tax treatment. The main core of the text dealt with depreciation and capital gains, exchanges and conversions, and tax treatment of various forms of ownership.[55] In general, the text emphasizes that the knowledge and familiarity with real estate taxation is the crucial factor in real estate investment analysis.

Higgins,[56] Wendt,[57] and Stauss[58] emphasized tax advantages and tax shelter benefits for real estate projects. Boyce and Higgins emphasized the importance of depreciation for the real estate investor.[59] A HUD study on taxation impacts reported a variety of effects on property markets.[60]

Smith, Tschappat, and Racster presumed that "income, state and gift taxes exert a great influence on real estate decisions."[61] Aronsohn concluded that it is a myth to consider real estate as a tax shelter since there are many more considerations that must be taken into account than simply considering the analysis of "investment in a machine."[62]

In 1974 Wyndelts examined the question of the relevance of tax planning for real estate investment. One major finding was that the use of marginal tax

Table1-1
Reasons for Investing in Real Estate

Reasons for Investing	*Percent of Type of Property*							
	Farm Land	*Urban Land*	*1-Unit Residential*	*2-4 Unit Residential*	*Apartment House*	*Commercial Property*	*Individual Property*	*Total*
Stability of value	10	7	6	7	14	6	18	8
Inflation hedge	13	9	10	14	5	10	12	10
Forced saving	8	5	12	11	9	15	18	11
Equity buildup	5	9	8	4	14	12	12	8
Bargain price	5	15	18	10	2	8		8
Rate of return		2	4	5	2	3	6	3
For improvement	5	5		1	5	4		3
Capital gain	21	32	12	12	9	9	12	13
Tax shelter	5		16	14	12	17	6	11
Self-employment	8		6	5	14	3		5
Control of investment	5	5	8	5	7	8	5	6
Advice of broker				1	2	2		1
Other	15	11		10	5	3	11	7
Blank				1				6
Total	100	100	100	100	100	100	100	100

Source: Irving F. Davis, Jr., *A Study of Real Estate Investment Returns to Capital and Management* (Fresno, Calif.: California State University Bureau of Business Research and Services, Study no. 14, July 1973), p. 80. Reprinted with permission.

rates in real estate investment analysis will tend to overstate rates of return compared to using the scheduled rate for the taxpayer.[63]

Cooper summarized the tax literature by suggesting that the major emphasis in real estate investment comes from emphasis on the following tax-related items: tax shelter, depreciation, capital gains calculations, interest deductions, and other taxes.[64] In general, most of the authors cited argued that tax planning and analysis is a crucial item in effective real estate analysis. Many presented reasons why the link between real estate and taxation is so important. However, few have been able to effectively demonstrate the relative importance of taxation over other considerations. For most of the writers, taxation was implicity assumed to be crucially important.

The Importance of Other Considerations for Real Estate

Some writers emphasized additional factors and their effect on real estate. It has traditionally been assumed that mortgage rate changes significantly affect property values and expected rates of return.[65] Kinnard demonstrated that a fifty basis point increase in the mortgage rate, when the rate is less than 6 percent, the impact on the equity yield rate would be ninety basis points, if the equity yield note was initially above 7 percent.[66] Thus, he suggested that debt financing and changes in financing terms have a substantial impact on value and can determine whether or not to invest in the project.

A recent address by Crean emphasized that monetary and fiscal policy considerations are very important for real estate development.[67] This discussion highlighted the impact of tight monetary policy, inflation objectives, the "crowding out" phenomenon in capital markets, and financial intermediary problems. He concluded that high interest rates hurt real estate markets but inflation also menaces rates of return in real estate. If tight monetary policy can dampen inflation, he suggested, the real estate market would be helped.[68]

In 1970, however, Gibbons observed that the impact of increased interest rates may be cushioned by the availability of tax-sheltered income. He also viewed the money markets as suppliers of an "abundance of funds [for] real estate equity investments in a market of limited opportunities."[69] While it is highly questionable as to whether capital flows are abundant for real estate, Gibbons makes a strong case for the necessity of favorable financing arrangements for investment decisions.

Nelson and Pollakowski provided some examples of the effect of financing on value but argued that the availability of refinancing enabled investors to hedge against further losses as a result of expected smaller cash flows.[70] They concluded that the size of the mortgage payment was an important consideration in periods of rising interest rates. Pyhrr also argued that sensitivity analysis can be used by lenders to examine the impact on value that various debt coverage ratios would have.[71] The implication is that lending arrangements are an important concern in real estate investment analysis.

Other writers emphasized additional variables as well. Hodges argued that the after-tax selling price less the unpaid mortgage (reversionary interest) was "often the largest factor determining equity yield."[72] Feinschreiber suggested that although rental income is the largest number on a project's financial statement, "rent roll analysis doesn't always receive attention proportionate to its numerical amount."[73] In his earlier study, Case provided possible explanations as to why returns were higher in the western United States. These included faster rates of urban growth and the lack of rent control among others.[74] Roulac emphasized that in land speculation, substantial holding period costs may occur so as to require a substantial rate of appreciation in order to achieve a normal return."[75] A recent series of articles centered on the determination of the optimal holding period determination.[76]

In general, depending upon who one reads, one can expect to find support for the importance of almost any factor over others in real estate decision-making. Most frequently, after tax considerations, these involve mortgage terms and rates, growth in the reversion, or optimal holding periods.

The Role of Property Management

Noticeably absent, or at least de-emphasized from much of the literature, is the role of management as a consideration in the investment process. There are a few exceptions to this statement, however. As early as 1936, interest was expressed in the management considerations in investment decision-making. Aldis pointed out his surprise at Babcock's statements concerning property management and real estate appraisal. Babcock's dismissal of the importance of management is evident in his citing of "numerous cases where office buildings succeed in spite of relatively poor management."[77] Babcock also suggested that management "does not usually affect the income-producing capacity of ordinary store properties" when they are strategically located.[78]

However, Ratcliff confirmed the link between real estate investment and management.

> The act of investing in real estate is only the first step toward the investment objectives which prompted the commitment of capital. To produce the expected net return, the real estate enterprise must be successfully and profitably operated as a business. Thus the investor is found with the diverse problems of managing the enterprise. . . .[79]

Davis studied the importance of property management in investment property. He was aware of the significance of managerial ability by warning that "ignorance and inexperience in management can lead to serious investment errors."[80] His study hypothesized that successful real estate ventures were characterized by contributions paid to management as well as capital. This so-called joint contribution would explain why management was so important and investment in real estate was insufficient to ensure success.[81]

This attitude was also brought forth in recent texts by Maisel and Roulac,[82] Messner, Schreiber, and Lyon,[83] and especially McMahan.[84] Although the emphasis in the first two is primarily the traditional accounting consideration, these three books indicate support for the proposition that management is significantly important. Maisel and Roulac described management as a "primary factor which must be examined to make good forecasts and proper decisions."[85] They pointed out that while substantial underestimates of development and operation costs may mean disaster for the project, the management firm has the responsibility of ensuring success. They suggested that the owner's ability to select good management, although variable among firms, will determine the bottom line or the ultimate success of the project.[86] Messner, Schreiber, and Lyon emphasized the role of management as well but failed to explain why "a sometimes neglected characteristic of real estate investment is the requirement of management."[87] With the exception of some basic considerations, this text fails to link management and investment analysis.

However, the most extensive argument can be found in McMahan. Although he emphasized tax advantages ("one of real estate's foremost attractions as an investment, is its favored tax status"), he devoted a considerable amount of space to the importance of good property management. He listed a number of reasons that cause developers to stay clear of management.

> Property management requires extraordinary attention to detail that most developers/investors would as soon avoid.
>
> Developers often are "new deal" oriented–impatient with the problems of a completed project and anxious to begin a new one.
>
> Investors often are passive, preferring not to get involved in day-to-day operations.
>
> Some aspects of property management (for example, janitorial services, trash removal, repairs) involve functions which many consider beneath their dignity.
>
> Many leases contain escalation clauses which tend to lull developers, investors into believing that they are totally protected against cost increases.[88]

Thus, he concluded, many real estate parties think property management is unimportant and relegate it to the back room. However, he warned:

> *And yet probably no other area of real estate has a more pronounced and continuing effect on the success of a project.* This is because:

> A reduction in operating costs can often significantly affect ROI. For example, a 10% reduction in operating costs can improve cash flow by as much as 25%.
>
> A properly serviced building will result in more lease renewals, thereby reducing turnover, vacancy and merchandising costs.
>
> A well-maintained building will result in prolonging the physical life of its components, thereby reducing repair costs and replacement frequency.
>
> A well-serviced and maintained building will command a greater price when the building is sold, all other factors being equal.[89]

McMahan suggested that the decision to manage the property personally or by an independent firm is a very important and fundamental one. His conclusion that necessarily followed was that "a manager can profoundly affect the continuing profitability of a successful building project" and therefore, by providing essential services, must be considered in the investment decision.[90]

Summary

The attraction of real estate for investors was examined in a number of ways. Historically, many of these types of analysis differed in approach and logic. Economically speaking, we can determine which factors are more significant than others. With more interest in real estate investment analysis, certain items appeared to be more important than others to numerous authors. More sophisticated analysis has enabled better identification of key variables.

The historical emphasis has clearly been placed on the impact that taxation and depreciation have had on real estate projects. Most of the traditional work emphasized these considerations. Other literature looked to the financing variables as important areas of analysis. A smaller set of writers concerned themselves with alternative items such as future selling prices or expected growth rates in selling prices or, most recently, holding period analysis.

However, one prominent consideration that seems to have been overlooked by most writers, is the role that property management plays in the property's operation. Specifically, the link between investment analysis and property management requires further development. A few authors have laid the groundwork for this investigation.

Traditional Methods of Investment

Methods of investment analysis have developed in recent years from a series of guidelines or rules of thumb to more sophisticated time-adjusted measures. As this development occurs, reexamination brings forth clearer definitions and new theoretical models.

This section reviews some of the traditional considerations in institutional investment analysis and examines some of the concerns about risk. Although reviewed extensively elsewhere in the past few years, a brief summary of the traditional models of capital budgeting is presented and related to real estate investment needs.

Theory of Investment

It is generally assumed that investment decisions are made according to some well-established criterion. However, the well-known goal of wealth maximization is usually not adopted in real-life decision-making. In light of the possibility of uncertain events and unclear criteria, Bridge and Dodds suggested that the necessary type of decision-making may not be based upon wealth maximization. They emphasized that a decision is basically making a choice among alternatives, and when uncertainty exists, it becomes increasingly difficult to select a criterion, alternative, or course of action.[91]

In a text devoted entirely to investment decisions, Bierman and Smidt argued that the "receipt or disbursement of cash [is the] crucial event" rather than the determination of income.[92] Although the use of cash flow valuation was suggested as early as 1930 by Wiese[93] and formally demonstrated in 1938 by Williams[94] for bond and stock valuation, much of the theory of investment for real estate analysis has failed to use such development.

In 1965 Graham presented six screening tests for real estate assets, which consisted of single-period measures of value, return, and coverage.[95] The investment analysis consisted of a comparison of the rules of thumb with average or normative tests. Presumably, real estate investment decision-making could be precise as a result of these comparisons.

Many writers have since pointed out the problems and inadequacies of the lack of a viable investment theory prior to the late 1960s. Cooper presented a list of single-period rules of thumb for investment value, cash down payment, purchase price, or expected rate of return.[96] He implied that these measures fail to treat many of the considerations which modern real estate analysis must consider, and thus these measures are obsolete.

Hysom and Juengling observed that increased competition for finance and land, and rising construction costs indicate "the old rules of thumb no longer apply and the margin for error must be reduced" in real estate investment analysis.[97] They advocated using standard time-adjusted measures of rate of return: net present value, return on investment, and the profitability index.

In two articles, Roulac listed sixteen alternative definitions of rate of return.[98] He stated that the real estate investment community may not know enough about real estate investment analysis to understand which rate of return is used when, and what the implications are for certain measures instead of others. In addition, he listed ten frequently used definitions of sales proceeds, three for financing, and eight for investment. The implication is that these concepts are far from universally understood.

Most writers have come to recognize that any potentially acceptable measure of investment value (or return) must treat at least four basic factors: time, uncertainties, risk and trade-offs between multiple objectives.[99] Hence, most definitions of investment value incorporate these considerations. Similar definitions have been proposed by Ratcliffe,[100] Boyce, [101] Smith, Tschappat, and Ratcliff, [102] Kinnard,[103] and others.

A paper by McNeeley presented an outline of the basic steps of economic analysis for real estate analysts.[104] These include (1) identifying income and expenses, (2) calculating the cash flow, (3) analyzing the tax effects, and (4) evaluating, with appraisal decision rules. While this outline is generally followed by all investment analysts, McNeeley further argued that the importance of the investment process can be found early in the analysis. Unrealistic presumptions about income or expenses will obviously result in inaccurate decision rules for the analyst.

Risk

Traditionally, risk, or "the chance of probability that the investor will not receive his expected or required rate of return,"[105] has not been effectively treated in investment analysis. There have been or remain a number of controversies in this area. Some of these are questions as to whether there is a difference between risk and uncertainty, the appropriate measure for risk, or the best methodology for evaluating investments in risky situations. While some of these considerations are treated later, it should be pointed out that traditionally risk was something which was known to exist, but writers generally failed to properly account for it.

Most traditional financial theory split total risk into business risk, or the uncertainty of the prediction of productivity of the investment, and financial risk, or the proportionate margin of safety before net operating income and the contract mortgage payments or debt service.[106]

Pyhrr observed that prior to risk analysis using probabilistic modeling techniques, risk was formerly treated in one of three ways: analysis of the payback period, use of a risk-adjusted discount rate, or conservatism in making estimates.[107] But in the end, Pyhrr suggested, the analysis of risk was left to the four horsemen of implicit decision-making: judgment, hunch, instinct, and intuition.[108]

Baumol observed that with modern developments, there are more available methods of treating risk than ever before.[109] He listed six methods: finite-horizon modeling method, risk-adjusted discount rates, the Shackle approach (a variation of the certainty-equivalent approach), probabilistic modeling, sensitivity analysis, and decision theory. Baumol indicated a preference for using risk-adjusted discount rates or sensitivity analysis since he found the others to be deficient or currently unavailable for real-world use.

Harrison argued that traditional single-point investment analysis implicitly deals with risk in that the riskiness of the variables are treated in the estimates. Thus the best traditional decision-making can do in terms of meaning or estimating risk is to provide intuitive analysis of projects.[110]

A recent paper by Curcio and Gaines examined various risk measures used in modern portfolio theory to security selection and evaluation.[111] After a review of the financial literature employing measures such as systematic risk, semivariance, skewness, kurtosis, and stochastic dominance, they concluded that most studies used a variance-type measure for risk. In the case of real estate, this was viewed as a considerable deficiency.

Traditional Models

Thorne provided a useful classification of measures of return.[112] He called the rules of thumb and other single-point measures first-generation measures of return and those treating the time value of money in the investment decision as second-generation techniques. He analyzed further development as well but argued that the second-generation models provided "a universal and unequivocal indication of investment criteria; namely the internal rate of return (IRR)."[113]

Others praised the IRR as well as net present value (NPV). Cooper's numerous objections to simpler models were satisfied by the IRR or NPV and while he carefully listed the many assumptions associated with these models, he advocated their use as investment tools.[114] Gibbons and Rushmore reviewed these methods and modified the IRR for explicit reinvestment specification.[115] Dilmore reviewed popular capitalization methods, all of which measured the time value of money.[116] Clettenberg and Kroncke[117] and Hawk and Kroncke[118] provided similar reviews.

Perhaps the best review can be found in Hemmer.[119] He listed ten reasons why the discounted cash flow approach was valuable. Among these reasons he included a better measure of return, establishment of predetermined investment criteria, better analysis of the project during the construction period, analysis of various financing packages, and enabling the analyst to perform sensitivity analysis.[120] In addition, he suggested that without this model, it would not be possible to describe accurately the interrelationships of the investment decision and thus derive a good measure of rate of return. Further, one could obtain optimal measures of depreciation, participation, and refinancing, if desired.

Moreover, with computerization, the model could be used without data specification and could substantially affect investment valuation abilities.[121]

Hax and Wiig provided a concise table of four leading investment methods: payback period, accounting rate of return, NPV, and IRR.[122] In discussing the advantages and disadvantages of each method, they attempted to account for the wide use of all the methods in real-world decision-making. However, the criticisms of many of these techniques have become well known. They suggested that in all cases, these measures transform cash flow into a simple profitability measure. The relevant consideration is which measure is the best one for use in capital investment, of which real estate is a special case.

Wendt and Tandy reviewed eight of the more well-known discounted cash flow models used in real estate.[123] Although some models employed slightly different assumptions, the authors found that those surveyed produced similar results, and so they encouraged the continued use of these models.

Summary

The lack of a theory of investment in real estate analysis has hampered developments in that area. However, capital theory in economics and capital budgeting in finance have made substantial headway in developing models, decision rules, and concepts. Prior to the late 1960s, investment analysis of real estate projects was primarily based upon single-period rules of thumb or simply intuition. The developments in finance led to the adoption of time-adjusted measures of return and value. Although far from completely understood, these measures have become part of the traditional literature in real estate investment analysis. Risk was discussed and its treatment in traditional modeling surveyed. In general, risk is a topic which has not been adequately treated, although newer developments have done slightly better. A short review of the traditional models was presented, with emphasis placed on the advantages and disadvantages of the major methods of analysis.

New Developments in Real Estate Investment Analysis

Since real estate investment analysis has developed rapidly over the past few years, a review of the new developments is warranted. Although there have been many diverse advancements, this section reviews and summarizes the more important areas of the future. While the primary emphasis is on computerization and probabilistic modeling, this section discusses some of the problems with the traditional theory and criticisms found in finance literature. In addition, various issues, such as risk and uncertainty, and the role of sensitivity analysis in attempting to measure risk are discussed. The argument on probabilistic versus deterministic models is presented and the section concludes by covering other recent developments in real estate investment theory and analysis.

The Necessity of New Theory

In recent years, many writers have found many deficiencies in the traditional models. Farrell observed three major problems with traditional analysis: limitations of single-period measures, omission of the treatment of the equity revision, and inconsistencies of many of the traditional criteria and methods.[124] While many of these considerations have been treated by computerization of traditional second-generation models, a number of problems remain for analysts.

Pellatt reached two similar conclusions at the beginning of his paper on probabilistic modeling.[125] He argued that the reliance upon rules of thumb for investment analysis was a characteristic of "almost all methods of analysis."[126] In particular, he cited the general use of gross income multipliers in that they are measures of return without consideration of present value techniques. In addition, he argued that although readily available in 1972, "virtually no methods of analysis apply sophisticated computational techniques or statistical tests of validity" for making real estate investment decisions.[127]

Pellatt examined discounted cash flow models or, as he called it, the "modified Inwood method," to ascertain whether this analysis could overcome the numerous shortcomings. He found it deficient on a number of points, including the limited use of the expected value operator for internal rate of return calculations, the interdependence of cash flows, the relationship between changes in income and changes in expenses, and the poor treatment of risk. Thus, Pellatt proceeded, as had Pyhrr independently, to examine a probabilistic approach to investment decision-making, advocating the superiority of such an approach to overcome these disadvantages by freeing the analysis from restrictive assumptions or by providing more information useful in the decision-making process.

Messner and Findlay also pointed out the deficiencies in traditional techniques. They cited two weaknesses inherent in traditional investment analysis: poor measures of performance and a failure to "account for the realities of the market place.[128] The poor measures include the standard ones—payback period and the IRR—and the other objections were failure to treat the timing of cash flows, the impact of financing, and the necessity to consider the impact of taxation. But their main objection was with the IRR.

After a discussion of the popularity of this measure and the standard discussion of the IRR's presumptions and limitations,[129] Messner and Findlay introduced a new measure of performance called the financial management rate of return (FMRR). Based upon a geometric mean calculation, the FMRR has been argued to be superior to the IRR by freeing it from its reinvestment assumptions by maximizing terminal wealth. A recent paper by Findlay, Messner, and Tarantello attempted to modify the probabilistic modeling of Pyhrr by using the FMRR calculation.[130]

Criticisms Found in Finance Literature

It has been argued and demonstrated that a knowledge of capital budgeting and financial decision-making is crucial for real estate investment analysis.[131] Since many of the developments in real estate investment analysis can be found in earlier writings, a knowledge of this literature is imperative for the real estate analyst. There are many areas of analysis where this contention seems to hold.

Financial leverage is a well-known concept in financial theory. Its impact on value and return has been extensively examined in corporation finance and recently in real estate. Hitchings provided a thorough demonstration of the effects of leverage on property for investment analysis and market-appraised values.[132] But warning of the costs attributed to holding land in speculation, Roulac in 1975 suggested that the availability of leverage for real estate speculators provides "probably the most mistaken view of risks and returns."[133]

While many writers suggested reasons for the use of mortgage loans in real estate development, few were able to demonstrate analytically the effect of leverage on the return to equity. White [134] and Gaumnitz[135] presented a formulation which shows the effect of financial leverage on the return to equity.

Both White and Gaumnitz found average returns for the periods they studied to be lower than expected, and therefore prone to negative leverage. White suggested that there may be other reasons why investors seek real estate, given the poor returns. These include tax shelter benefit and disenchantment with the stock market and other alternative investments, but mostly refuge from inflation in recent years.[136] The important implication here is that the measurement of rate of return as a goal for investors even after treating for leverage appears to be questionable, given the poor results, and investment continues to increase.

Another area of analysis is the treatment of uncertainty in a deterministic investment model. As indicated previously, some writers preferred to treat risk and uncertainty by adjusting the discount rate accordingly or by adopting a conservative attitude in analyzing the project. Robichek and Myers advocated the use of an alternative approach in accounting for risk and uncertainty: the certainty-equivalent approach.[137] They argued that the uncertainty of the cash flows may not be a function of time and thus by adjusting the level of the discount rate to reflect increased uncertainty, one implies that uncertainty does vary with time. Furthermore, they suggested that if this uncertainty was not constant over time, the problem could not be solved without simulation of the future cash flows, since no information would be available and therefore investors would lack a strategy without such information.[138] Thus, under the certainty-equivalent approach, the cash flows would be treated for uncertainty while the rate of discount would be free from this consideration.

A later Robichek and Myers paper argued the theoretical superiority of the certainty-equivalent approach and concluded that the analysis of uncertainty with respect to time is crucial if one wishes to use a risk-adjusted discount rate. If uncertainty is resolved over time, a constant discount rate may be used. But if this is not possible, the use of a risk-adjusted discount rate would be inappropriate.[139]

A few writers examined the modern techniques of analysis (IRR and NPV) with rules of thumb. Schwab and Lustig examined the NPV and the profitability index or benefit-cost ratio as economic criteria for desision-making.[140] After an analysis of net versus gross ratios, the authors chose to use the net ratio. In addition, they highlighted some of the limitations of the use of a benefit-cost ratio for investment analysis.

Sarnat and Levy examined the relationship of well-known rules of thumb to the IRR as measures of approximation.[141] They found that for proposals with holding periods of less than three years, the accounting rate of return on total investment provided a closer approximation of IRR, independent of the value of the IRR, than did the accounting rate of return on average investment. They also found that for IRR values greater than 20 percent, the accounting rate of return on total investment provided a closer approximation of IRR, independent of the duration of the holding period, than did the accounting rate of return on average investment.[142] Although the authors warned that "even minor deviations of the rules of thumb from the internal rate imply possible uncompensated departures from optimality," they showed that the payback method and the two accounting return measures are acceptable approximations, depending upon the size of the IRR and the length of the holding period.

Real Estate and Computerization

Much of the current interest in real estate investment analysis can be linked to developments in the computerization of real estate return calculations. Walters, in his collection of readings titled *Real Estate Computerization,* attempted to survey the important articles in the literature of real estate and computerization.[143] His book contains articles in six major areas of real estate: property management, appraisal, investment analysis, marketing, land value forecasting, and the future of real estate. The collection emphasized the potential of computerization in many areas of real estate analysis.

Dasso also wrote a monograph describing computers and computer usage in real estate.[144] While general in nature and content, this work emphasized that the future of real estate analysis lies in computerization.

A recent monograph by the Institute of Real Estate Management examined the question of whether or not the property management firm should be computerized.[145] They concluded that computerization may be an improvement and a justified expenditure if the cost is feasible to the company.

While many writers listed the benefits of computerization, Cooper and Pyhrr emphasized that the major advantage of computerization is that it gives the user the ability to identify varied situations in calculating rates of return.[146] In fact, as implied by Cooper and Pyhrr, computerization has enabled a more general use and understanding of sensitivity analysis as a technique in real estate investment. This, of course, is the primary focus of this work.

In a series aimed at demonstrating the variety of computer applications, Shenkel presented computer models for a discounted cash flow model, an equity-capitalization (Ellwood) adaptation, an example using multiple regression to predict value, and an application of leasehold valuation.[147] While these articles serve mostly as demonstrations of techniques, it should be apparent that the computer can serve as an aid in decision-making for a variety of purposes. In concluding, Shenkel predicted that computerization will be a helpful tool for real estate analysts by increasing their efficiency and thereby increasing the value of their services.[148]

As an exemplification of the potential forms of analysis available with computerization, Poorvu and Stevenson presented an example where the rankings of hypothetical projects varied according to investment criteria used.[149] They concluded that the computer ought to provide so much more information about making an investment that it would serve as a major tool for analysts.

Probabilistic Modeling

The famous article by Hertz[150] opened new avenues for investment analysis. Since the understanding of uncertainty and risk is to understand the key business problem and the key business opportunity, Hertz provided the probabalistic framework for investment of capital projects. He observed that the reason deterministic discounted cash flow methods fail was because "the estimates used in making the advanced calculations are just that—estimates."[151] Thus, with the use of a Monte Carlo simulation, Hertz demonstrated how more information could be obtained and evaluated prior to the investment decision. Pyhrr's major contribution was the adaptation of Hertz's model to real estate investments.[152]

Pouliquen argued that probabilistic modeling (risk analysis) was an effective method of dealing with uncertainty since it enabled the analysis to be performed over the entire possible range of outcomes and associated a likelihood or occurrence for each value.[153] The well-known discrete three-point input approach used by many writers in real estate investment analysis was, for Pouliquen, a form of sensitivity analysis. However, as demonstrated in a later section, for other writers, the low-middle-high approach was a form of risk analysis.

Pyhrr argued that a true risk analysis must use a probabilistic model.[154]

In addition, he pointed out that various writers have used sensitivity testing to measure what they termed risk. But sensitivity analysis could not technically be termed risk analysis since a likelihood function is not available with sensitivity analysis.[155] Pyhrr concluded by suggesting that a risk simulation model "can help decision-making to accumulate and weigh information about risk characteristics of proposals and perhaps avoid unwise investments," and can provide positive side effects of increased education about real estate investment analysis.[156]

Singer linked probabilistic modeling to appraisal techniques.[157] He argued that the appeal of probabilistic models rests in their ability to make information more available and thus comparisons between alternative investments more meaningful. He concluded by suggesting that risk analysis aids in minimizing overall risk rather than improving definitions of value.

Probabilistic modeling is becoming well known in real estate circles. Although it was used in other industries more than fifteen years ago,[158] the real estate industry has just begun to understand and use these models. Maisel and Roulac briefly discuss Monte Carlo techniques for real estate investment.[159] Pyhrr and McKinnon recently prepared a probabilistic model that provides information as to which properties brokers should concentrate on over others in terms of their sales potential.[160] Finally, the paper by Findlay, Messner, and Tarantello sought to improve Pyhrr's original probabilistic model by simulating returns of the FMRR.[161] They concluded by summarizing the controversy of the FMRR and the IRR, and suggested that simulating FMRRs would improve investment decision-making.

Additional Considerations

The question of whether one is concerned about risk or uncertainty is a very old one. The original distinction comes from Knight's famous *Risk, Uncertainty and Profit.*[162] Whereas most writers tend to view the concepts of risk and uncertainty interchangeably in finance as well as real estate,[163] a few have maintained the distinction. While the distinction between risk and uncertainty may often appear to be unimportant, Baumol supports Knight's original categorization. If there is an element of uncertainty in the outcomes, this element can be referred to as risk or uncertainty. If these outcomes can be predicted or estimated, then this is risk. If not, uncertainty is present.[164] Bridge and Dodds[165] and MacCrimmon[166] provided similar definitions and maintained the distinction. However, Raper stated that "risk is a proxy for uncertainty."[167]

Quirin[168] and Grayson[169] argued that the distinction of whether the probability distribution is known or unknown is obsolete. If decision makers have some feel for the likelihood of some event occurring but most likely do not know the probabilities associated with each event, the terms can be used synonomously.[170] This led Pyhrr to join the bandwagon and he defined risk as "the probability of not receiving the expected or required rate of return."[171]

However, Pyhrr also stated that deterministic modeling cannot truly measure risk. He implied that deterministic models and the discrete three-point approach, which is really the twice-repeated use of the deterministic model under two sets of assumptions or the multiple use of the deterministic model under multiple sets of assumptions (sensitivity analysis), cannot be classified as risk analysis since the assumptions selected are not based upon any probabilities of occurrence. If the user can associate probabilities with the selection of inputs, the model becomes probabilistic in design. If the user cannot derive or estimate probabilities for those inputs, the model remains deterministic (that is, one cannot perform risk analysis). However, the three-point approach may tell us more than a two-point approach or a single-point estimate. And similarly, a complete sensitivity analysis may provide more information about the likelihood of returns or values, varying under certain assumptions, than an incomplete analysis. Sensitivity analysis tells us about uncertainty: the uncertainty of expected outcome.

Therefore, this argument suggests that the traditional distinction between risk and uncertainty may be trivial in some cases, but in the case of real estate modeling proves to be a significant factor. With this distinction, one can observe that risk analysis is possible only with probabilistic models and is not possible, as some writers have suggested, with sensitivity analysis or the common three-point method. If a probabilistic model is not used, one cannot say anything about the riskiness of the project; one can, however, provide some information as to how well the project will do in light of uncertain forces that would cause the project to reach optimistic or pessimistic estimates. If the user can estimate the probability associated with optimistic or pessimistic results, the process becomes probabilistic again, since some probability can be associated with the outcome, in the jargon of Knight.

A related consideration is the interest in the discrete three-point method mentioned earlier. As implied above, there have been many misconceptions about the use of the optimistic-most likely-pessimistic approach. (This approach has been called a variety of things: low-most probable-high, very favorable-most favorable-least favorable, high-base-low, three-step approach, three-value approach, and no doubt others.)

Many writers advocated its use as an important technique or as a partial form of sensitivity analysis;[172] others believed that this technique was something else. Bridge and Dodds implied that the three-step approach was probabilistic modeling.[173] Wright said this method "approaches risk analysis."[174] Cooper and Morrison[175] and Montgomery[176] argued that this method was a technique of sensitivity analysis but both argued sensitivity analysis could be used to measure risk. Ratcliff and Schwab argued this approach was close to a probabilistic model and thus risk analysis, except they maintained that their probabilities were arbitrarily chosen and they did not know what distribution to use in the analysis.[177]

Miles and Pyhrr attempted to justify use of this deterministic method but maintained that the model was for "risk analysis and risk management."[178] They suggested four reasons: ease of working with it compared to probabilistic methods, ease of understanding for practitioners, flexibility of use, and general use by other writers. None of these reasons seems satisfactory enough for the adoption of this technique as a proxy for risk analysis.

But Pouliquen stated best the relationship between sensitivity analysis and probabilistic modeling. After stating that he believed this approach to be a sensitivity analysis, he pointed out that "one does not sources of uncertainty."[179] However, with many variables, sensitivity analysis is not a viable technique since the different combinations of variables are so large.

Deterministic versus Probabilistic Models

The purpose of the above arguments is to clarify the relationships between deterministic and probabilistic modeling. While probabilistic modeling directly deals with risk and deterministic modeling cannot, the author is not convinced of the superiority of probabilistic modeling in all cases. A controversy has erupted over the question of which type of model is preferred for capital investment analysis.

An important article by Lewellen and Long suggested that deterministic modeling is as useful as probabilistic modeling.[180] The development of the latter, it has generally been assumed, is superior both theoretically and operationally. They argued their case based upon five issues: rate of return calculation, variability of project life, asymmetrical outcomes, interdependencies among cash flows, and a portfolio problem.

In essence, they found that the mean of the distribution of internal rates of return was lower than the deterministic, single-point estimate of internal rate of return.[181] They also examined the effects of uncertainty about the duration of the cash flow and found the expected value of the cash flow stream was different than the value of the expected (deterministic case). Additional analysis found problems with the use of model values, demand schedules, and a capital market issue.

However, on the basis of most of their findings, they concluded that single-point estimates may be just as valuable or greater than those derived in a probabilistic approach if the latter is costly or difficult to use.[182] Therefore, they regarded simulation as an unnecessary technique.

Three comments appeared in response to Lewellen and Long's article. One takes issue with only the fifth item but agrees with the four presented here.[183] A comment by Bower and Lessard defended risk analysis by arguing that the firm gains some information using probabilistic analysis and that management does not have enough information to make as effective decisions as possible.[184] Gentry also suggested that additional information is the key to risk analysis by arguing that the information provided by risk analysis could provide new insights into the valuation process.[185] Most of Gentry's criticism, however, centered upon objections to the capital market implications.

Lewellen and Long replied that they would continue to regard single-value discounted cash flow analysis as better operational approximation than simulation and that the comments confuse the point of investment analysis: the decision point is at the time the decision is being made, and not five periods after the analysis has taken place.[186] Furthermore, the authors viewed the simulation process as unclear and under certain conditions may prove to be too much of an approximation to be very useful.

Therefore, one can conclude that while probability modeling has some appeal and attraction, certain theoretical problems as well as noted operational constraints exist with its use. If one is aware of the limitations and appropriate uses of deterministic investment models, their use will remain very effective. In light of criticisms of probabilistic modeling, deterministic modeling may remain a highly useful approach for years to come.

Other Developments

For some, the contribution of Ellwood's capitalization rate was a major development in 1957. In summarizing traditional rate of return models, Cooper suggested that there are at least four reasons why Ellwood is an improvement: use of average income for the holding period only, mortgage financing arrangements are considered, measurement of return on equity, and residential value would be estimated rather than fixed.[187] Kinnard's income property text extensively uses Ellwood for investment decision-making.[188] Maes viewed Ellwood as more of an investment analysis tool rather than a method of market valuation.[189] In the same light, Wendt showed that the returns calculated using Ellwood, Inwood, and the IRR are identical, given some basic input assumptions.[190] This important finding suggested that the interest in Ellwood may have been overstated since alternative methods of analysis may provide similar results. Shenkel[191] and Dasso, Kinnard, and Messner[192] provided computerization for the Ellwood technique. While each is different in perspective, they illustrate possibilities of computerized use of this alternative approach.

Following the work of Swalm,[193] Ratcliff and Schwab[194] developed a decision theory model for real estate based upon cardinal utility theory, as originally proposed by von Neumann and Morgenstern in their *Theory of Games and Economic Behavior.* Ratcliff and Schwab took Swalm's model and adapted it for investment in real estate. Thus, "each individual attempts to optimize the expected value of something which is defined as utility, and that for each individual a relationship between utility and dollars can be found."[195] This is one area where more research needs to be done.

Another recent development is modeling that has attempted to overcome shortcomings of the IRR. Two such concepts are Messner and Findlay's FMRR[196] and Friedman's pull factor.[197] While the authors disagreed as to the worth of each other's technique,[198] both attempted to improve upon the results in the investment decision. In the case of the FMRR, a geometric mean rate of return is calculated instead of the IRR, which frees it from many constraints and enables optimal holding period analysis to take place. With the pull factor, Friedman argued additional information is provided as a guide as to whether or not the investor should hold or sell in any given year. However, when funds are rationed, Messner and Findlay argued that mathematical programming must be used to solve the problem.[199] The paper by Findlay and Howson determines the optimal holding period using dynamic programming.[200]

Three other papers are also worth mentioning. Roulac identified the three-phase investment cycle and argued that better investment decisions are possible if one examines the life cycle of a real estate investment.[201] While the emphasis was placed on tax consequences and financing effects, Roulac suggested a new framework of analysis for real estate investment.

Curcio and Gaines have begun to investigate the portfolio theory applications for real estate.[202] Although Friedman attempted to link real estate investment analysis and portfolio theory in 1970,[203] his initial work has been shown to be severely lacking. Little work has been done in this area since that time.

Hettenhouse and Dee argued that real estate investment analysis can actually be viewed as a component analysis of rate of return.[204] In addition to the traditional two components of cash flow and changes in property value at time of reversion and the returns from the reinvestment of cash flows, they argued that two other components ought to be valued: Changes in the capitalized value of the mortgage indebtedness and the entrepreneurial return.[205] They also presented empirical results which indicated various rates of return, depending upon how many of the five components are explicitly valued.

Summary

Developments in real estate investment analysis have been extensive in the past decade. Much of the new development has come about as a result of reexamination of the traditional real estate theory and practice; however, a large part can be attributed to developments in theoretical finance. Examples such as leverage, the certainty-equivalent approach, and testing of rules of thumb have appeared in the finance literature.

Computerization has enabled real estate investment analysis to become a quantitative area. Analysis has become very exact and "doing it by the numbers" appeared to dominate more traditional analyses. Probabilistic modeling attempted to improve upon risk measurement and assessment.

Other areas of interest include the risk versus uncertainty question, the overuse of three-point estimation models, and the controversy of the alleged superiority of probabilistic over deterministic models. Other developments include the Ellwood technique, decision theory applications, and attempts at improving decision criteria.

An Overview of the History of Real Estate Investment

This chapter has reviewed the history of real estate investment analysis by examining reasons why investors chose real estate, which variables have been regarded as important in making decisions, traditional methods of measuring returns and value, and newer developments in investment theory. In general, a lack of agreement exists among real estate writers on many issues. This can be supported by the wide range of opinions and recommendations found in this review. Furthermore, in terms of the importance attached to various considerations in the investment decision, the variables chosen vary substantially according to the source used. Recent developments and controversies cited in this chapter suggest that much interest has been generated in the area of real estate investment decision-making, although many of the newer developments are either well established in other disciplines but not well known among real estate writers or are very recent real estate findings and as yet are not fully accepted.

This extensive review summarized the history of investment valuation thought and thereby demonstrated the lack of consensus among the profession. It also demonstrated the varied emphasis found in the literature regarding the major variables thought to be crucial in the investment decision. In addition, it has updated the field by reviewing recent developments in investment theory and modeling.

The survey provides the primary foundation for this study by thoroughly demonstrating a major reason for its conception; since the literature has failed to agree upon which variables are crucial in the investment decision even among similar criteria, a study needs to be done to satisfy this concern. The wide range of considerations demonstrated here suggests that to a large extent, the real estate profession has not understood which variables are most crucial in effective decision-making. This exhaustive review serves as a testimonial to the urgency and importance of a complete sensitivity analysis for real estate investors as proposed in chapter 4.

Notes

1. See Halbert C. Smith and Ronald L. Racster, "Should the Traditional Appraisal Process Be Restructured?," *The Real Estate Appraiser* 36 (November/December 1970): 6-11; Paul F. Wendt, "Recent Developments in Appraisal Theory," *The Appraisal Journal* 37 (October 1969): 485-500; Richard U. Ratcliff, "Is There a 'New School of Appraisal Thought?' " *The Appraisal Journal* 40 (October 1972): 522-528; idem, "Appraisal *Is* Market Analysis," *The Appraisal Journal* 43 (October 1975): 485-490.

2. Frederick M. Babcock, *The Valuation of Real Estate* (New York: McGraw-Hill Book Co., 1932), p. 440.

3. See Edwin S. Mills, "The Value of Urban Land," in *The Quality of the Urban Environment,* ed. by Harvey S. Perloff (Baltimore, Md.: Johns Hopkins Press, 1969), pp. 231-253; Robert F. Muth, "The Derived Demand for Urban Residential Land," Urban Studies 8 (October 1971): 243-254; J.F. Kain and J.M. Quigley, "Measuring the Value of Housing Quality," *Journal of the American Statistical Association* 65 (June 1970): 532-548; Michael J. Ball, "Recent Empirical Work on the Determinants of Relative House Prices," *Urban Studies* 10 (1973): 213-233; D.M. Grether and P. Mieszkowski, "Determinants of Real Estate Values," *Journal of Urban Economics* 1 (April 1974): 127-146.

4. See M.D. Nourse, "The Effect of Air Pollution on Housing Values," *Land Economics* 43 (May 1967): 181-189; Robert J. Anderson, Jr., and Thomas D. Crocker, "Air Pollution and Residential Property Values," *Urban Studies* 8 (October 1971): 171-180; Ronald G. Ridker and John A. Henning, "The Determinants of Residential Property Values with Special Reference to Air Pollution," *Review of Economics and Statistics* 49 (May 1967): 246-257; E.P. Seskin, "Residential Choice and Air Pollution: A General Equilibrium Model," *American Economic Review* 63 (December 1973): 960-967; K.F. Wieand, "Air Pollution and Property Values: A Study of the St. Louis Area," *Journal of Regional Science* 13 (April 1973): 91-95.

5. See J.P. Crecine, O.A. Davis, and J.E. Jacson, "Urban Property Markets: Some Empirical Results and Their Implications for Municipal Zoning," *Journal of Law and Economics* 10 (October 1967): 79-99; J.A. Bruna, "Zoning—Its Effect on Property Value," *The Appraisal Journal* 37 (October 1969): 555-561; Frederick H. Rueter, "Externalities in Urban Property Markets: An Empirical Test of the Zoning Ordinance in Pittsburgh," *Journal of Law and Economics* 16 (October 1973): 313-350.

6. See Wallace E. Oates, "The Effect of Property Taxes and Local

Public Spending on Property Values: An Empirical Study of Tax Capitalization and the Tiebout Hypothesis," *Journal of Political Economy* 77 (November/December 1969): 957-971; Frederick D. Stocker, "Effects of Taxation on Urban Land Use," *The Appraisal Journal* 39 (January 1971): 57-69; D.N. Hyman and E.C. Rasour, Jr., "Real Property Taxes, Local Public Services, and Residential Property Values," *Southern Economics Journal* 39 (April 1973): 601-611; E.M. Sabella, "The Effects of Property Taxes and Local Public Expenditures on the Sales Prices of Residential Dwellings," *The Appraisal Journal* 42 (January 1974): 114-125.

7. Sherman J. Maisel and Stephen E. Roulac, *Real Estate Investment and Finance* (New York: McGraw-Hill Book Co., 1976), p. 6.

8. Ibid.

9. R. Bruce Ricks, *Recent Trends in Institutional Real Estate Investment*, Research Report, no. 23 (Berkeley, Calif.: University of California, Center for Real Estate and Urban Economics, Institute of Urban and Regional Development, 1964), p. 2.

10. Ibid., p. 5.

11. Ibid.

12. Ibid., p. 87.

13. Halbert C. Smith, "Investment Analysis in Appraising," *The Real Estate Appraiser* 33 (September 1967): 19-25.

14. Smith and Racster, "Traditional Appraisal Process," p. 7.

15. Ibid., p. 8.

16. James A. Graaskamp, "A Practical Computer Service for the Income Approach," *The Appraisal Journal* 37 (January 1969): 50-57.

17. Lloyd D. Hanford, "The Use of Discount Cash Flow Analysis," *The Real Estate Appraiser* 39 (November/December 1973): 31-34.

18. John Grey Peatman, "The Psychology of Real Estate Investments," *The Appraisal Journal* 10 (October 1942): 335.

19. E.W. Bedford, "Why Buy Real Estate?" *The Appraisal Journal* 13 (April 1945): 135.

20. Ibid.

21. Ibid.

22. Ibid., p. 137. The quote is reprinted with permission. The opinions and statements set forth herein do not necessarily reflect the viewpoint of the American Institute of Real Estate Appraisers or its individual members, and neither the Institute nor its editors and staff assume responsibility for such expressions of opinion or statements.

23. James D. Landauer, "Real Estate as an Investment," *The Appraisal Journal* 28 (October 1960): 426-434.

24. Ibid., p. 434.

25. Ibid., p. 428.

26. Ibid., pp. 428-429.

27. Sanders A. Kahn, Frederick E. Case, and Alfred Schimmel, *Real Estate Appraisal and Investment* (New York: Ronald Press, 1963).

28. Leo Grebler, *Experience in Urban Real Estate Investment* (New York: Columbia University Press, 1955).

29. Ibid., p. 7. See also Wallace F. Smith, *The Low-Rise Speculative Apartment,* Research Report, no. 25 (Berkeley, Calif.: University of California, Center for Real Estate and Urban Economics, Institute of Urban and Regional Development, 1964), p. 81.

30. Grebler, *Urban Real Estate,* pp. 7-8.

31. Ibid., p. 24.

32. Fred Case, "Comparative Real Estate Investment Experience," *The Appraisal Journal* 28 (July 1960): 337-344.

33. Ibid., pp. 339, 342.

34. S.L. Hayes and L.M. Harlan, "Real Estate as a Corporate Investment," *Harvard Business Review* 45 (July/August 1967): 9.

35. Smith, *Low-Rise Speculative Apartment,* p. 9.

36. Ibid., p. 101.

37. Anthony Downs and M. Leanne Lachman, "The Current Climate for Real Estate Investment and Development," *Real Estate Review* 4 (Spring 1974): 29.

38. Ibid.

39. U.S. Department of Housing and Urban Development, *Study on Tax Considerations in Multi-Family Housing Investments,* HUD contract H-1227 (May 7 1971), prepared by Touche, Ross and Co., p. 4. See also Arnold H. Diamond, "Motivations of Investors in Multifamily Housing," *The Real Estate Appraiser* 38 (May/June 1972): 17-24.

40. HUD, *Multi-Family Housing Investments,* p. 9

41. Irving F. Davis, *A Study of Real Estate Investment Returns to Capital and Management* (Fresno, Calif.: California State University Bureau of Business Research and Services, Study No. 14, July 1973).

42. Robert J. Wiley, "Real Estate Investment Analysis: An Empirical Study," *The Appraisal Journal* 44 (October 1976): 586-592.

43. Ibid., p. 592.

44. National Institute of Farm and Land Brokers, *Federal Taxes Affecting Real Estate* (Chicago: National Institute of Farm and Land Brokers of the National Institute of Real Estate Brokers, 1970), p. 1.

45. Alan R. Cerf, *Real Estate and the Federal Income Tax* (Englewood Cliffs, N.J.: Prentice-Hall, 1965), pp. 1-3.

46. Paul F. Wendt and Alan R. Cerf, *Real Estate Investment Analysis and Taxation (New York: McGraw-Hill Book Co., 1969).*

47. J. Warren Higgins, Impact of Federal Taxation on Real Estate Decisions, Report no. 11 (Storrs, Conn.: Center for Real Estate and Urban Economic

Studies, 1971); idem, "Impact of Federal Taxation on Real Estate Decisions," *The Appraisal Journal* 40 (January 1972): 32-41.

48. Paul F. Wendt, "Cash Flow Analysis by Computer," *Real Estate Review* 2 (Fall 1972): 68.

49. Byrl N. Boyce and J. Warren Higgins, "Tax Shield Considerations in Real Estate Investment Decisions," *The Real Estate Appraiser* 39 (November/December 1973): 39-44.

50. HUD, *Multi-Family Housing Investments;* idem, *Housing and Federal Taxation: Costs and Effectiveness,* June 19, 1973.

51. Halbert C. Smith, Carl J. Tschappat, and Ronald L. Racster, *Real Estate and Urban Development* (Homewood, Ill.: Richard D. Irwin, 1973), p. 326.

52. Robert W. Wyndelts, "Tax Planning and an Analysis of Federal Income Tax Laws: Investment Decisions in Real Estate" (Ph.D. dissertation, University of Georgia, 1974).

53. John McMahan, *Property Development–Effective Decision Making in Uncertain Times* (New York: McGraw-Hill Book Co., 1976), p. 256.

54. Cerf, *Real Estate,* p. 2.

55. Wendt and Cerf, *Real Estate Investment,* pp. 69-162.

56. Higgins, *Impact of Federal Taxation, p. 15.*

57. Wendt, "Cash Flow Analysis," p. 68.

58. George Stauss, "The Effect of Tax on Yield and Value," *The Appraisal Journal* 37 (July 1969): 393.

59. Boyce and Higgins, "Tax Shield Considerations," p. 38.

60. HUD, *Housing and Federal Taxation,* p. 1.

61. Smith, Tschappat, and Racster, *Real Estate,* p. 326.

62. Alan J.B. Aronsohn, "The Myth of Real Estate as a Tax Shelter," *Real Estate Review* 3 (Summer 1973): 59.

63. Wyndelts, "Tax Planning."

64. James R. Cooper, *Real Estate Investment Analysis* (Lexington, Mass.: Lexington Books, D.C. Heath and Co., 1974), pp. 3-4.

65. Smith, Tschappat, and Racster, *Real Estate,* p. 100.

66. William N. Kinnard, Jr., *Income Property Valuation* (Lexington, Mass.: Lexington Books, D.C. Heath and Co., 1971), pp. 150-151.

67. Michael J. Crean, "Commentary: Monetary and Fiscal Policies: Their Impact on Real Estate," *The Real Estate Appraiser* 42 (March/April 1976): 56-57; also in *Journal of Property Management* 41 (March/April 1976) 64-65.

68. Ibid., p. 57.

69. James E. Gibbons, "Impact of Yields on Value," *The Appraisal Journal* 38 (October 1970): 508.

70. Roland D. Nelson and Arthur J. Pollakowski, "The Effect of Financing on Value," *The Appraisal Journal* 40 (April 1972): 279-283.

71. Stephen A. Pyhrr, "Analytical Methods Can Reduce Income Property Loan Losses," *The Real Estate Appraiser* 41 (March/April 1975): 39

72. M.B. Hodges, Jr., "Computer Progress in Valuation of Income Properties," *The Appraisal Journal* 39 (January 1971): 20.

73. Robert Feinschreiber, "A Practical Approach to Rent Roll Analysis," *Real Estate Review* 5 (Summer 1975): 96.

74. Case, "Comparative Real Estate Investment," p. 344.

75. Stephen E. Roulac, "Anatomy of a Land Deal," *Real Estate Review* 4 (Winter 1975): 96.

76. M. Chapman Findlay, III, and Hugh R. Howson, "Optimal Intertemporal Real Estate Ownership, Valuation and Use," *American Real Estate and Urban Economics Association Journal* 3 (Summer 1975): 51-66; Stephen D. Messner and M. Chapman Findlay, III, "Real Estate Investment Analysis: IRR Versus FMRR," *The Real Estate Appraiser* 41 (July/August 1975): 5-20; Jack P. Friedman, "The Internal Rate of Return Plus the Pull Factor," *The Real Estate Appraiser* 42 (March/April 1976): 29-31; M. Chapman Findlay, III, Stephen D. Messner, and Rocky A. Tarantello, "An FMRR Simulation Model" (paper presented at Financial Management Association Meetings, Montreal, Quebec, October 1976).

77. Graham Aldis, "Management as a Factor in Appraisal," *The Appraisal Journal* 4 (April 1936): 188-189.

78. Ibid.

79. Richard U. Ratcliff, *Real Estate Analysis* (New York: McGraw-Hill Book Co., 1961), p. 211. (Copyright © 1961, McGraw-Hill, Inc. Used with permission.)

80. Davis, *Real Estate Investment Returns,* p. vii.

81. Ibid.

82. Maisel and Roulac, *Real Estate,* pp. 6-7.

83. Stephen D. Messner, Irving Schreiber, and Victor L. Lyon, *Marketing Investment Real Estate* (Chicago: Realtors National Marketing Institute of the National Association of Realtors, 1975), pp. 17-18.

84. McMahan, *Property Development,* pp. 351-370.

85. Maisel and Roulac, *Real Estate,* p. 6.

86. Ibid., p. 7.

87. Messner, Schreiber, and Lyon, *Marketing Investment,* p. 24.

88. McMahan, *Property Development,* p. 352. (Copyright © 1971 by McGraw-Hill, Inc. Used with permission of McGraw-Hill Book Co.)

89. Ibid., pp. 352-353. See note 88.

90. Ibid., p. 370.

91. J. Bridge and J.C. Dodds, *Managerial Decision Making* (New York: John Wiley and Sons, 1975); p. 16.

92. Harold Bierman, Jr., and Seymour Smidt, *The Capital Budgeting Decision,* 3d ed. (New York: Macmillan Co., 1971), p. 27.

93. Robert F. Wiese, "Investing for True Values," *Barron's* (September 8, 1930): 5.

94. John Burr Williams, *The Theory of Investment Value* (Cambridge, Mass.: Harvard University Press, 1938).

95. Donald H. Graham, Jr., "Owner's Analysis of Yields on Major Real Estate Investments," *The Appraisal Journal* 33 (October 1965): 542.

96. Cooper, *Real Estate,* pp. 12-13.

97. John Hysom and Charles Juengling, "Computerized Cash Flow Analysis," *Urban Land* 29 (October 1970): 161.

98. Stephen E. Roulac, "Truth in Real Estate Reporting," *Real Estate Review* 3 (Spring 1973): 91; idem, "The Promoter's Participation Interest as a Form of Compensation in Real Estate Syndication," *The Real Estate Appraiser* 39 (May/June 1973): 34.

99. Arnoldo C. Hax and Karl M. Wiig, "The Use of Decision Analysis in Capital Investment Problems," *Sloan Management Review* 17 (Winter 1976): 19.

100. Ratcliff, *Real Estate Analysis,* p. 119.

101. Byrl N. Boyce, ed., *Real Estate Appraisal Terminology* (Cambridge, Mass.: Ballinger Publishing Co., 1975), P. 118.

102. Smith, Tschappat, and Racster, *Real Estate,* pp. 95-99.

103. Kinnard, *Income Property Valuation,* pp. 13-15.

104. W.S. McNeeley, "Money-making in Real Estate Is a Numbers Game," *Real Estate Review* 2 (Spring 1972): 14.

105. Stephen A. Pyhrr, "Real Estate Risk Analysis Goes Scientific," *Real Estate Review* 2 (Fall 1973): 63.

106. Ratcliff, *Real Estate Analysis,* p. 116. Similar definitions can be found in Paul M. Van Arsdell, *Corporation Finance* (New York: Ronald Press Co., 1968), pp. 301-304; Stephen A. Pyhrr, "A Computer Simulation Model to Measure Risk in Real Estate Investment," *The Real Estate Appraiser* 39 (May/June 1973: 15; and *American Real Estate and Urban Economics Association Journal* 1 (June 1973): 51.

107. Pyhrr, "Computer Simulation Model," p. 15.

108. Ibid., p. 13.

109. William J. Baumol, *Economic Theory and Operations Analysis,* 3d ed. (Englewood Cliffs, N.J.: Prentice-Hall, 1972), pp. 477-483.

110. Ian W. Harrison, *Capital Investment Appraisal* (London: McGraw-Hill Book Co., 1973), p. 66.

111. Richard J. Curcio and James P. Gaines, "The Measurement and Analysis of Risk in Real Estate Investment" (paper presented at the Southern Finance Association Meetings, Atlanta, Ga., November 1976).

112. Oakleigh J. Thorne, "Real Estate Financial Analysis—The State of the Art," *The Appraisal Journal* 42 (January 1974): 7-37.

113. Ibid., p; 36.

114; Cooper, *Real Estate,* pp. 14-21.

115. James E. Gibbons and Stephen Rushmore, "Using Total Project Analysis to Compete for Investment Capital," *The Appraisal Journal* 43 (October 1975): 491-502.

116. Gene Dilmore, "Internal Rate of Return and the Reinvestment Concept," *The Real Estate Appraiser* 39 (July/August 1973): 29-31.

117. Karel J. Clettenberg and Charles O. Kroncke, "How to Calculate Real Estate Return on Investment," *Real Estate Review* 2 (Winter 1973): 107-109; idem,) "A Note on Equity Costs in Real Estate Investments," *The Appraisal Journal* 39 (October 1971): 535-539.

118. Stephen L. Hawk and Charles O. Kroncke, "Some Refinements in the Real Estate Investment Decision Process," *The Real Estate Appraiser* 40 January/February 1974): 13-19.

119. Edgar H. Hemmer, "How a Computer 'Thinks' About Real Estate," *Real Estate Review* 4 (Winter 1975): 113-123.

120. Ibid., p. 114.

121. Ibid., p. 119.

122. Hax and Wiig, "Use of Decision Analysis," pp. 26-27.

123. Paul F. Wendt and Janet Tandy, "Evaluation of DCF Computer Models in Real Estate Investment Analysis," rev. ed., Athens, Ga., April 1976, pp. 12-20 (Mimeographed).

124. Paul B. Farrell, "Computer-Aided Financial Risk Simulation," *The Appraisal Journal* 37 (January 1969): 65.

125. Peter G.K. Pellatt, "The Analysis of Real Estate Investments Under Uncertainty," *Journal of Finance* 27 (January 1972): 459.

126. Ibid.

127. Ibid.

128. Messner and Findlay, "Real Estate Investment Analysis," pp. 5-6.

129. For reviews of thc problems with the IRR, see Dilmore, "Internal Rate of Return," pp. 29-38, and Joseph Strung, "The Internal Rate of Return and the Reinvestment Presumptions," *The Appraisal Journal* 44 (January 1976): 23-33. See also Austin J. Jaffe, "Is There a 'New Internal Rate of Return Literature?'" (Working Paper, University of Illinois at Urbana-Champaign, 1977). for a critique and review of much of this writing.

130. Findlay, Messner, and Tarantello, "An FMRR Simulation Model."

131. Jaffe, "Rate of Return Literature."

132. T.C. Hitchings, Jr., "Leverage," *The Real Estate Appraiser* 39 (May/June 1973): 42.

133. Roulac, "Anatomy of a Land Deal," p. 93.

134. John R. White, "How Real Estate Decisions Are Made," *Real Estate Review* 5 (Fall 1975): 43-44.

135. Jack E. Gaumnitz, "Analyzing Rates of Return on Real Estate Investments" (Lawrence, Kans.: University of Kansas, Working Paper no. 107 1976), pp. 2-4.

136. White, "Real Estate Decisions," pp. 45-46.

137. Alexander A. Robichek and Stewart C. Myers, *Optimal Financing Decisions* (Englewood Cliffs, N.J.: Prentice-Hall, 1965), p. 80. See also James C. Van Horne, *Financial Management and Policy,* 3d ed. (Englewood Cliffs, N.J.: Prentice-Hall, 1974), pp. 133-160.

138. Robichek and Myers, *Optimal Financing Decisions,* p. 141.

139. Alexander A. Robichek and Stewart C. Myers, "Note: Conceptual Problems in the Use of Risk-Adjusted Discount Rates," *Journal of Finance* 21 (December 1966): 730.

140. Bernhard Schwab and Peter Lustig, "A Comparative Analysis of the Net Present Value and the Benefit-Cost Ratio as Measures of the Economic Desirability of Investments," *Journal of Finance* 24 (June 1969): 507-516. See also G. David Quirin, *The Capital Expenditure Decision* (Homewood, Ill.: Richard D. Irwin, 1967), pp. 46-49.

141. Marshall Sarnat and Haim Levy, "The Relationship of Rules of Thumb to the Internal Rate of Return: A Restatement and Generalization," *Journal of Finance* 24 (June 1969): 479-490.

142. Ibid., p. 485.

143. David W. Walters, ed., *Real Estate Computerization,* Research Report, no. 35 (Berkeley, Calif.: University of California, Center for Real Estate and Urban Economics, Institute of Urban and Regional Development, 1971).

144. Jerome Dasso, *Computer Applications in Real Estate,* Real Estate Report, no. 13 (Storrs, Conn.: Center for Real Estate and Urban Economic Studies, 1974).

145. Institute of Real Estate Management, *Computer Applications in Property Management Accounting* (Chicago: Institute of Real Estate Management, 1975).

146. James R. Cooper and Stephen A. Pyhrr, "Forecasting the Rates of Return on an Apartment Investment: A Case Study," *The Appraisal Journal* 41 (July 1973): 313.

147. For the cash flow model, see William M. Shenkel, "Cash Flow Analysis: An Application of Conversational Computer Programming," *Journal of Property Management* 34 (July/August 1969): 165-72. For an Ellwood adaptation, see William M. Shenkel, "Equity-Capitalization and Investment Decisions: An Application of Conversational Computer Programming," *Journal of Property Management* 34 (March/April 1969): 76-87. For use with multiple regression analysis, see William M. Shenkel, "Cash Flow Analysis and Multiple Regression Techniques: A Computer Application of Apartment Properties," *Journal of Property Management* 34 (November/December 1969): 264-276. For a model to value leaseholds, see William M. Shenkel, "Net Ground Lease Analysis for Decision Making Purposes," *Journal of Property Management* 35 (March/April 1970): 76-87.

148. Shenkel, "Net Ground Lease Analysis," p. 79.

149. William J. Poorvu and Howard H. Stevenson, "Making the Right Real Estate Bet," *Real Estate Review* 5 (Winter 1976): 61-64.

150. David B. Hertz, "Risk Analysis in Capital Investment," *Harvard Business Review* 42 (January/February 1966): 95-106.

151. Ibid., p. 105.

152. Originally presented in Stephen A. Pyhrr, "A Proposed Model to Simulate Internal Rate of Return and Risk Characteristics of Investments in Multi-Family Rental Housing" (Ph.D. dissertation, University of Illinois at Urbana-Champaign, 1972).

153. Louis Y. Pouliquen, *Risk Analysis in Project Appraisal* (Baltimore, Md.: Johns Hopkins Press, 1970), p. 2.

154. Pyhrr, "Real Estate Risk Analysis," p. 65.

155. Pyhrr, "A Proposed Model," pp. 192-193.

156. Pyhrr, "Real Estate Risk Analysis," p. 67.

157. Bruce Singer, "New Methods of Income Analysis," *The Appraisal Journal* 39 (July 1971): 327-337.

158. For a good review, see Pyhrr, "A Proposed Model," pp. 204-205, 219-223. See also C. Jackson Grayson, Jr., *Decisions Under Uncertainty: Drilling Decisions by Oil and Gas Operators* (Boston: Division of Research, Harvard Business School, 1960), and John H. Norton, "The Role of Subjective Probability in Evaluating New Product Ventures," *Chemical Engineering Symposium Series #42, Statistics and Numerical Methods in Chemical Engineering* (New York: American Institute of Chemical Engineers, 1963).

159. Maisel and Roulac, *Real Estate,* pp. 405-410.

160. Stephen A. Pyhrr and H. Alexander McKinnon, "Development and Implementation of a Linear Programming Model for Optimally Allocating Real Estate Brokerage Activity" (paper presented at Financial Management Association Meetings, Montreal, Quebec, October 1976).

161. Findlay, Messner, and Tarantello, "An FMRR Simulation Model," pp. 1-5.

162. Frank H. Knight, *Risk, Uncertainty and Profit* (Boston: Houghton Mifflin, 1923).

163. Of finance writers, Hertz, "Risk Analysis," p. 105; Van Horne, *Financial Management,* p. 133; Bierman and Smidt, *Capital Budgeting Decision,* p. 109; and others. Of real estate writers, Gibbons and Rushmore, *Total Project Analysis,* p. 502; Singer, "Income Analysis," p. 337; Raymond L. Erler, Rate of Return and Financial Leverage: A Paradigm for Sensitivity Analysis," *The Appraisal Journal* 40 (July 1972): 369; J. Thomas Montgomery, "Real Estate Investment Risk—Basic Concepts," *The Appraisal Journal* 44 (January 1976): 20; Maisel and Roulac, *Real Estate,* p. 405.

164. Baumol, *Economic Theory,* p. 574.

165. Bridge and Dodds, *Managerial Decision Making,* p. 277.

166. Kenneth R. MacCrimmon, "Descriptive and Normative Implications

of the Decision-Theory Postulates," in *Risk and Uncertainty,* ed. by Karl Borck and Jan Mossin (London: Macmillan and Co., 1968), pp. 11-12.

167. Charles F. Raper, "Internal Rate of Return—Handle with Care," *The Appraisal Journal* 44 (July 1976): 409.

168. Quirin, *Capital Expenditure Decision,* p. 199.

169. C. Jackson Grayson, Jr., "The Use of Statistical Techniques in Capital Budgeting," in *Financial Research and Management Decisions,* ed. by Alexander A. Robichek (New York: John Wiley and Sons, 1967), pp. 90-132.

170. Ibid., p. 91.

171. Pyhrr, "A Proposed Model," p. 175.

172. National Institute of Farm and Land Brokers, *Federal Taxes,* p. 339; Smith, Tschappat, and Racster, *Real Estate,* Edward F. Gallagher, "Sensitivity Analysis for Apartment House Investment Property," in *Real Estate Computerization,* ed., Walters, p. 192; Messner, Schreiber, and Lyon, *Marketing Investment,* p. 264.

173. Bridge and Dodds, *Managerial Decision Making,* pp. 280-281.

174. M.G. Wright, *Discounted Cash Flow* (London: McGraw-Hill Publishing Co., 1967), p. 135.

175. James R. Cooper and Cathy A. Morrison, "Using Computer Simulation to Minimize Risk in Urban Housing Development," *The Real Estate Appraiser* 39 (March/April 1973): 15-26.

176. Montgomery, "Real Estate Investment Risk," p. 20.

177. Richard U. Ratcliff and Bernhard Schwab, "Contemporary Decision Theory and Real Estate Investment," *The Appraisal Journal* 38 (April 1970): 176.

178. Mike Miles and Stephen A. Pyhrr, "A Framework and Computer Model for Risk Analysis and Risk Management in Real Property Development" (paper presented at the Financial Management Association Meetings, Montreal, Quebec, October 1976).

179. Pouliquen, *Risk Analysis,* pp. 10-12.

180. Wilbur G. Lewellen and Michael S. Long, "Simulation Versus Single-Value Estimates in Capital Expenditure Analysis," *Decision Sciences* 3 (October 1972): 19-33.

181. Ibid., pp. 19-21.

182. Ibid., p. 29.

183. James Mandel and Wayne J. Morse, "Simulation Versus Single Value Estimates in Capital Expenditure Analysis: A Comment and Analysis" (Working Paper, University of Illinois at Urbana-Champaign, 1973).

184. Richard S. Bower and Donald S. Lessard, "The Problem of the Right Rate: A Comment on Simulation Versus Single-Value Estimates in Capital Expenditure Analysis," *Decision Sciences* 4 (October 1973): 571.

185. James A. Gentry, "Simulation Revisited," *Decision Sciences* 4 (October 1973): 572.

186. Wilbur G. Lewellen and Michael S. Long, "Reply," *Decision Sciences* 4 (October 1973): 575-576.

187. Cooper, *Real Estate,* p. 13.

188. Kinnard, *Income Property Valuation,* p. 285.

189. Marvin A. Maes, "Market Analysis and the Income Approach," *The Appraisal Journal* 44 (October 1976): 582.

190. Paul F. Wendt, "Ellwood, Inwood and IRR," *The Appraisal Journal* 35 (October 1967): 561-574.

191. Shenkel, "Equity Capitalization," pp. 76-87.

192. Jerome J. Dasso, William N. Kinnard, Jr., and Stephen D. Messner, "Lender Participation Financing: Applications of Sensitivity and Investment Analysis," *The Real Estate Appraiser* 37 (July/August 1971): 33-40.

193. Ralph O. Swalm, "Utility Theory–Insights into Risk Taking," *Harvard Business Review* 44 (November/December 1966): 123-138.

194. Ratcliff and Schwab, "Contemporary Decision Theory," pp. 165-187.

195. Swalm, "Utility Theory," p. 124.

196. Messner and Findlay, "Real Estate Investment Analysis," pp. 5-20.

197. Friedman, "Internal Rate of Return," pp. 29-31.

198. See Stephen D. Messner and M. Chapman, III, "Real Estate Investment Analysis: IRR + Pull Factor v. FMRR: A Comment," *The Real Estate Appraiser* 42 (July/August 1976): 58; Jack P. Friedman, "IRR + Pull Factor v. FMRR: AReply," *The Real Estate Appraiser* 42 (July/August 1976): 58-60.

199. Messner and Findlay, "Real Estate Investment Analysis," p. 19.

200. Findlay and Howson, "Real Estate Ownership," pp. 51-66.

201. Stephen E. Roulac, "Life Cycle of a Real Estate Investment," *Real Estate Review* 4 (Fall 1974): 113-117.

202. Richard J. Curcio and James P. Gaines, "Intertemporal Investment Revision: The Case of the Pure Real Estate Portfolio" (paper presented at the Financial Management Association Meetings, Montreal, Quebec, October 1976).

203. Harris C. Friedman, "Real Estate Investment and Portfolio Theory," *Journal of Financial and Quantitative Analysis* (April 1970): 861-874.

204. George W. Hettenhouse and John J. Dee, "A Component Analysis of Rates of Return in Real Estate Investment," *American Real Estate and Urban Economics Association Journal* 4 (Spring 1976): 7-22.

205. Ibid., p. 9.

2 The Contribution of Management Science to Decision-Making

Management science is a discipline that has been frequently criticized for failing to make its methodological results operational for users. However, in the area of investment decision-making, great strides have been taken which have substantially helped managers to better conceptualize their problems, calculate the results, and analyze the implications.

This chapter outlines the basic concepts of problem solving fundamentally important to operations research and management science. It reviews concepts of theories, models, and their relationships to real-world problems. Decision analysis is also introduced as an important area for real estate analysts to understand. While the treatment is very brief and introductory, the implication is that these areas should be more closely linked together than they have been in the past. Finally, simulation and sensitivity analysis is reviewed as discussed in management science literature. This discussion may clarify some of the misconceptions of these techniques that have carried over into real estate, finance, and other areas.

Basic Concepts of Scientific Problem Solving

Fundamentals of Operations Research and Management Science

Riggs and Inoue defined operations research as the "science devoted to the study of the behavior of man made systems" and management science as "the science that deals with the application of operations research techniques to management problems."[1] However, others have had difficulty distinguishing between these disciplines or even defining this field of study. Woolsey preferred a more loosely constructed definition by suggesting that this field relates logic and mathematics such that the methodology "does not get in the way of common sense."[2]

Since most writers have failed to develop working definitions for management science, they have had to be satisfied with descriptions and lists of characteristics in surveying the area. Furthermore, it may make little difference, whether one is talking about operations research or management science since the two are so closely related.[3]

Wagner identified four distinguishing characteristics of an operations research approach.[4] These include a primary interest on decision-making, the use of an economic effectiveness criterion, reliance upon a mathematical formulation, and an overall dependence upon a computer. He also viewed benefits of the operations research approach: better decisions, better management coordination, better control, and a better system. But perhaps his emphasis on model building as "the essence of the operations research approach" was Wagner's most inciting comment.[5]

Hammond listed six potential benefits for managers using management science.[6] Each of these would improve management's ability to make decisions, which, according to Simon, is the main function of management. As early as 1960, Simon stated that "decision making is synonymous with managing," [7] and therefore managers need to understand the science of making decisions: management science.

The operations research approach has been numerated by a number of writers. Ferber and Verdoun,[8] Ackoff,[9] and Naylor and Burdick[10] presented steps for designing and conducting operations research experiments. Each began with a clear formulation of the problem into a hypothesis or mathematical model. The next step generally involved deriving a solution to the model and testing the results. Finally, interpretation of the data and analysis of the results concluded the methods. Naylor, a leader in this field, also specified that the methodology of computer simulation could be easily formulated in this framework.[11]

Riggs and Inoue stated that a solution must satisfy the TAPE criterion (that is, *t*echnologically feasible, *a*dministratively convenient, *p*olitically expedient, and *e*conomically viable).[12] While they failed to discuss the importance of each of these considerations, they implied that all were necessary to arrive at a proper solution.

Using a similar approach, Harrison emphasized the necessity of an interdisciplinary framework for decision-making.[13] He suggested that a complete (or systems) analysis of the decision problem is an essential framework for analysis. He argued that many disciplines have a direct influence on the decision-making process, although often these disciplines tend to be excluded by the decision maker. Figure 2-1 illustrates Harrison's approach to the analysis of the environment on the decision-making process.

Teichroew argued that the decision-making process in management science relies chiefly on the mathematical formulation of problems.[14] Figure 2-2 is Teichroew's well-known model of the process of decision-making.

Comments on the Nature of Operations Research

In 1972, Mjosund reviewed the development of operations research over the prior thirty years and observed that the main forces had shifted from problem solving to methodology.[15] He called for more applications of techniques for

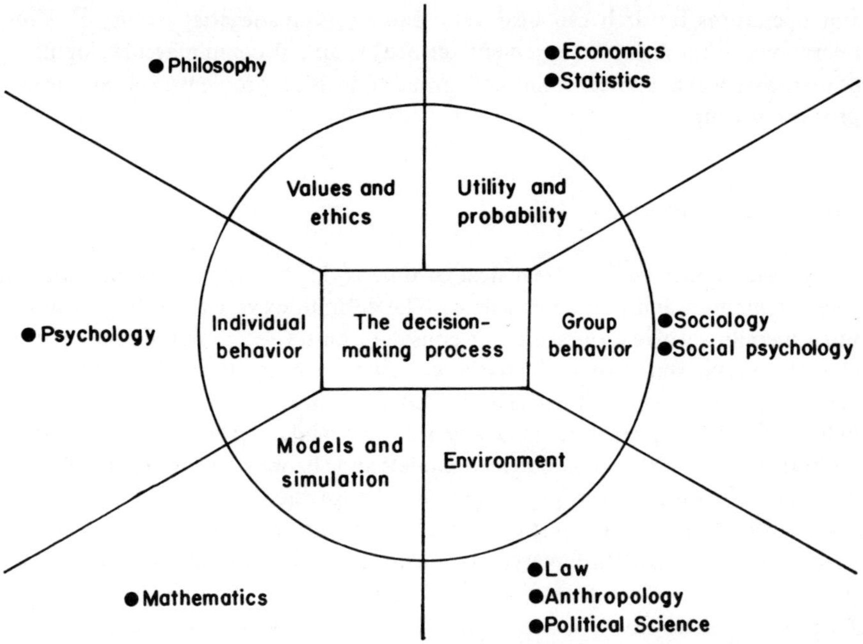

Source: F. Frank Harrison, *The Managerial Decision-Making Process* (Boston: Houghton Mifflin Company, 1975), p. 41. Reprinted by permission.

Figure 2–1. The Interdisciplinary Framework for Decision-Making

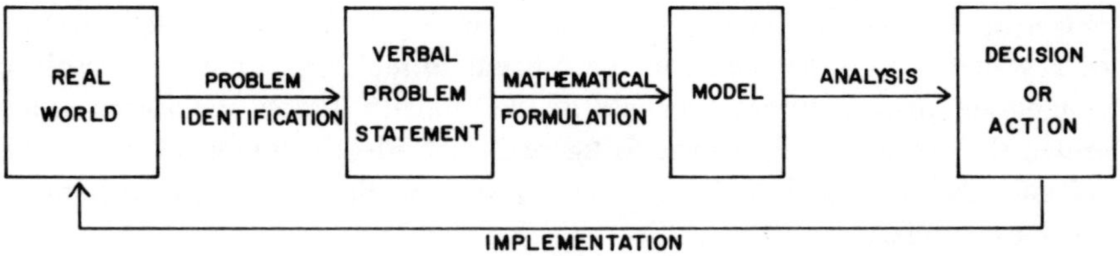

Source: Daniel Teichroew, *An Introduction to Mangement Science–Deterministic Models* (New York: John Wiley and Sons, 1964), p. 3. Reprinted with permission.

Figure 2–2. Mathematical Formulation of Problems

other disciplines. He concluded that without such use, operations research tools would fail to be useful for managers since it would be difficult to distinguish it from pure mathematics.

Simon and Newell as well as Mjosund, Wagner, Roccaferrera, and others recognized the importance of computers for operations research. With recent technical developments, these authors felt at that time and most likely even more so today, that in making complex decisions the tools of mathematics and operations research can bear very directly on managerial activity.[16] Thus, operations research (or management science) is an aid combining developments of mathematical analytics, computerization of decision problems, and managerial problem solving.

Theories and Models

Many writers have spent a great deal of time trying to explain the purposes and roles of theories and models in science. The definitions vary according to author but generally revolve around similar considerations. Crecine stated that a theory should contain statements of relationships between variables in the behavioral system.[17] But many authors have tended to emphasize the modeling of social behavior. This has resulted in a key role for models in social science. Some authors see little difference between models and theories. Singleton and Tyndall and others find these terms practically interchangeable.[18]

Another matter of interest concerns the reasons or purposes for constructing theories (or models). Durbin argued that there are two distinct goals of science—prediction and understanding—and each goal requires a separate framework. Prediction relates to reducing the differences between actual behavior and expected outcomes. To gain a basic understanding of social processes necessitates a solution to one prediction problem.[19]

Baumol,[20] Rigby,[21] and Naylor and coworkers[22] expressed similar reasons for the use of models. Horowitz emphasized that an alternative purpose for the use of models might be to generate new ideas. He suggested that although the model itself might not be very illuminating, it may lead to better identification of key factors or refinements in the original formulation, or it may result in elimination of superfluous elements of the model.[23] Carter and Hazan represented the use of models similar to figure 2-3.[24] While it is more complete and general, Carter and Hazan's depiction is very similar to the contentions of previous writers.

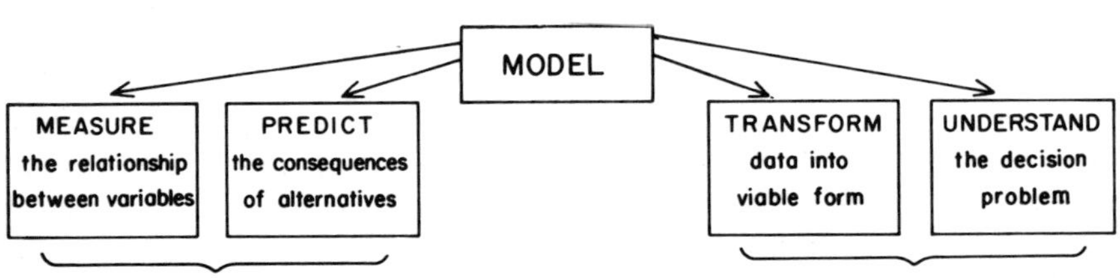

Source: L.R. Carter and E. Hazan, *A Practical Approach to Computer Simulation in Business* (New York: John Wiley and Sons, 1973), p. 25. Reprinted with permission of George Allen & Unwin.

Figure 2-3. The Uses of Models in Operations Research

The Relationship of Models to Reality

Wagner stated that "the model is a vehicle for arriving at a well-structured view of reality."[25] Boot emphasized that the assumptions of the model form the basis of the model, but the model's value rests on the degree to which its assumptions portray reality.[26] Gordon viewed the modeling process as one of gathering information for the purpose of studying the system of interest.[27] In the case of real-world phenomena, the model must provide information about reality.

Bross represented the relationship of model building to real-world understanding.[28] He emphasized that the quality of the model as judged by the evaluation phase is a very important concern if one wishes to learn about reality. As Gorry said, "a poor model may cause a manager to solve a problem poorly or [he may] solve the wrong problem."[29]

Little suggested that managers must understand the models they are using so they will know what to expect from them. He observed that models were not widely used by managers for three reasons: good models were hard to find, good parameterization of accepted models was even more difficult, and managers do not understand the models they were asked to use.[30]

Problems with Modeling Behavior

One of the most crucial problems is the ability to identify the problem that the user wishes to solve. Similar problems exist as far as limiting the problem in scope; but in terms of successful problem solving, the formulation of a model which directly and efficiently solves a problem is very important. Emshoff and Sisson suggested that the most critical step in model development is problem formulation.[31]

Simon listed the advantages of formulating problems mathematically. These include perceiving the mechanisms and relationships precisely, discovering postulates that can be derived from others and thereby eliminate unnecessary assumptions, discover inconsistencies in theory and empirical research, enable further elaboration of theory, and aid in handling complicated relationships.[32] While these general observations imply that mathematical problem solving is very advantageous, the problems associated with implementation may be substantial. Even if one knows exactly what the problem is, one must understand the model's implications and the empirical verification tests as well as the value of the model as a practical tool. This was perhaps best summarized by Chorafas in 1965 when he emphasized that a mathematical model must be easy enough for user manipulation and understanding, representative enough of the system, but complex enough to portray accurately that system.[33]

A number of authors have pointed out the necessity of limiting or abstracting the important factors from all considerations to solve problems. Bierman, Bonini, and Hausman, for example, noted this consideration as foremost in problem solving.[34] They urged decision makers to limit their data collection to those areas which are most relevant to their problem. In essence, they argued that "abstraction is the first and a necessary step in the solution of any human problem."[35] Schlaifer referred to a similar problem as the necessity of "delimiting" his decision. In particular, Schlaifer felt that analysis of a problem beyond some calculation date is not worthwhile since the effects of various acts are unknown in the present. Thus the decision maker must delimit by selecting a relevant planning period.[36]

In warning of the failure to abstract a model in search of a more realistic representation, Hillier and Lieberman warned of the dangers of such a decision. They suggested that the overly realistic model may result in a great deal of input preparation and processing to obtain only a small amount of information. Such a procedure may also obscure the significance of the important results.[37]

Wasson argued that effective decision-making cannot preclude qualitative analysis in light of recent moves toward better quantitative modeling. His perspective summarized the necessity of judgment and intuition in a reasonable quantitative analysis by relating both levels of analysis to making decision choices.[38]

Introduction to Decision Analysis

Foundations of Decision Analysis

In 1968, North stated that "decision theory was a way of formalizing common sense."[39] Furthermore, he described its value for potential decision makers by elaborating on its benefits: provides a logical framework in forcing the decision maker to rely upon his own judgment. But Howard, perhaps the father of decision analysis, stated that the ultimate limitation of decision analysis is not in its ability to logically solve problems, but in man's desire and search for logical solutions.[40]

The link between decision analysis and Bayesian cardinal utility decision-making is a strong one. The roots of decision analysis extend to von Neumann and Morgenstern's famous work, *Theory of Games and Economic Behavior.*[41] Other classic works have appeared by Pratt, Raiffa, and Schlaifer[42] and Edwards.[43] In addition, after having the foundations laid by von Neumann and Morgenstern, many applications have appeared that used their framework of analysis.[44]

Howard also provided a formal procedure for decision analysis. Although outlined in an earlier paper,[45] he divided decision analysis into three phases: deterministic, probabilistic, and post-mortem. Each aspect has a distinct role in providing a "logical basic for decision making in the face of uncertainty."[46]

A few observations are in order. First, Howard's decision analysis follows the tradition of the operations research approach to problem solving. In that respect, it is also a systems approach. Second, it clearly presents the roles of deterministic and probabilistic modeling, an aspect, as previously indicated, that is not clearly understood in economic and business research.

Third, given these two considerations, this analysis points out the role that each of these phases has in investment decision-making. Thus, deterministic modeling is only the beginning of the investment process rather than an end in itself. Similarly, probabilistic modeling is necessarily based upon deterministic inputs and cannot be freed of the deterministic analysis.

Finally, using Howard's work, one can see how sensitivity analysis fits into the overall framework of decision-making. Howard said that the "sensitivity of the best decision and its present value to the discount rate representing time preference would be an obvious test to perform."[47] An implication of this study could be that sensitivity testing in real estate investment analysis has been less obvious than Howard suggested.

Some Additional Considerations

Eilon suggested that what is meant by a decision is often overlooked or taken for granted. He argued that a decision is often thought to mean resolution or the determination of selection criteria as the crux of a decision. But he preferred to think of decision-making as relying upon the entire decision process before acting.[48]

Howard defined a decision as "an irrevocable allocation of resources, irrevocable in the sense that it is impossible or extremely costly to change back to the situation that existed before making the decision."[49] Thus, anytime a choice must be made by the decision maker and the outcome of the choice is important in that it is costly to revoke or it is irrevocable, and his welfare is affected by the choice, a decision must be made.

Others have observed some problems about decision analysis. Raiffa listed six problems with decision analysis as a method: too detailed to explain, implication that specifications are precise, necessity of complete quantification, nature of the analysis is to "divide and conquer" complex problems into simpler ones, decision analysis requires explicit articulation of thought processes, and decision analysis focuses only on quantifiable problems.[50]

White discussed the problems of establishing criteria for decision-making.[51] However, after highlighting those difficulties, he emphasized that in a dynamic world, criteria are changing so they must reflect changes that have occurred. But White stated that the big problem of decision analysis is "to achieve a workable and useful degree of isolation" of the process under study. Once the decision maker can do this, he knows enough to make correct decisions.[52]

Other writers have classified decision-making in different contexts. Luce and

Raiffa[53] and Richmond[54] distinguished decision-making according to the degree and type of certainty the user possessed. Ebert and Mitchell classified decision problems by outcome preferences and cause-and-effect relationships, where each determined a different strategy.[55] Arrow argued that decision theory is relevant only in the latter part of the structure of a decision problem: objective, policy alternatives, model specification, and computational methods.[56]

The Theory of Simulation Methods

Origins and Misunderstandings

The origins of what Wagner has called a "method of last resort" began in engineering and the physical sciences over fifty years ago. Lord Kelvin allegedly used a method of Monte Carlo analysis in 1901, although it was not referred to by that name.[57] It had not appeared until much later in economics or business research. Many authors tend to regard the origin of modern simulation methods as the development and use of Monte Carlo methods by von Neumann, Ulam, and Fermi during World War II and during the development of the atomic bomb.[58]

Rivett implied that simulation was regarded less favorably than more analytical approaches. However, he viewed the process as a changing one; while formerly the simulator tended to use this method in "a rather secretive fashion", since use and reliance implied some mathematical ineptitude, now it is the mathematician who must excuse himself for not using simulation.[59] Rivett conceded that inevitably the use of simulation models relied upon an act of faith by the user but warned that nearly all operations research techniques implied similar acts of faith, and that as long as the points at which faith was necessary were clear, simulation could be a valuable technique for behavior science.[60]

Naylor and coworkers suggested that the process of simulating has come into vogue to such a substantial extent that many confuse it with model building or computerization.[61] Tocher observed that "almost every model is hailed as a simulation" since its recent popularity, and many attempts at defining it have failed.[62] Teichroew and Lubin characterized problems solved by simulation techniques as "mathematically intractable and having resisted solution by analytic methods," typically involving many variables and parameters, mathematical functions that are not well behaved, and random variables.[63] However, Naylor described deterministic simulators as those that have stochastic variables suppressed.[64] Many others so defined simulation models as to include only those with random variables.

Many regard the use of computer models (whether deterministic or probabilistic) as evidence of simulation. For example, Jones described the necessity of computer access for simulation techniques by generalizing that "any simulation problem which can be solved without employing the computer can be solved without using the technique of simulation at all."[65]

The term "computer model" has been generally regarded as a distinct concept from simulation. Chacko distinguished between computerization and simulation. One major difference is that simulation requires the replication of the system as a whole so as to arrive at the composite picture.[66] In his discussion of various models, Rigby rejected the term computer model as a useful concept since it conveyed little information except that some type of model had been computerized.[67] He concluded that simulation was a distinctly different approach from model building, although some aspects of the two are similar.

Definitions of Simulation

As indicated previously, many authors have attempted to define simulation. These range from formal to operational definitions. It would be fair to suggest that a generally accepted definition has yet to be found.

Mize and Cox defined simulation as a standard methodology for studying systems or, more formally, as "the process of conducting experiments on a model of a system in lieu of either (1) direct experimentation with the system itself, or (2) direct analytical solution of some problem associated with the system."[68] Mao defined the technique "for evaluating the merits of alternative courses of action through experimentation performed on a mathematical model representing the actual decision-making situation."[69] Naylor, Burdick, and Sasser suggested that simulation was "a numerical technique for conducting experiments with certain types of mathematical and logical models describing the behavior of an economic system on a digital computer over extended periods of time."[70]

A widely recognized formal definition of simulation is credited to Churchman. He stated that x simulates y if and only if (1) x and y are formal systems, (2) y is a real system, (3) x is an approximation to the real system, and (4) the rules of validity in x are nonerror free.[71]

In general, a simulation can be characterized as a method of systems analysis which describes the systems' activity under study, using a model which, although not analytical, often provides comparable or superior information in the instances where analytical solutions are not possible.

Other Considerations

Naylor, Burdick, and Sasser also pointed out the importance of experimental design and simulation experiments. In arguing that design considerations have been ignored by economists modeling economic systems, they identified the difference between actual developments and simulations as the use of a model for experimentation in simulation rather than the actual system.[72]

As to the relationship of simulation to theory, Fleisher argued that simulation can help to develop theories by enabling the user to theorize. He maintained simulation could also help to avoid excess theorizing as well.[73] In fact, Dawson cited the general problem in simulation and modeling as the ability to adequately reproduce the real system theoretically. He emphasized the necessity of "abstracting from reality those components and relationships which are . . . crucial to what is being modeled."[74]

In general, simulation techniques have taken giant strides forward in helping to analyze problems. These arguments have not come without problems, Godin[75] and Goldie[76] highlighted some additional problems. Simulation, as a method of analysis, can be helpful to solve some problems, but harmful or misleading for others. The implication of this discussion has been that a knowledge of operations research concepts, including simulation, is an important concern for capital investment decision makers.

Sensitivity Analysis and Simulation Techniques

Sensitivity Analysis as a Technique in Operations Research

This technique is widely known in operations research, although generally not as highly regarded as in financial or real estate analysis. Van Horn[77] and Bentz, Sherr, and Miller[78] argued that sensitivity analysis was helpful in providing management with essential information at lower costs than could be derived empirically. Maffei suggested that sensitivity analysis should be used only as a guide. It can only suggest when to be wary of certain findings and should never be regarded as a panacea.[79] This approach has not always been taken by analysts in business research.

In economics, the use of comparative static analysis is very similar to sensitivity analysis. Baumol suggested that comparative statics could be used to "investigate the effects of a change . . . by comparing only the equilibrium positions before and after the change."[80] Certainly sensitivity analysis attempts to accomplish the same goal.

Sensitivity Analysis and Its Relationship to Simulation

Despite much research, the relationship between sensitivity analysis and simulation is not clear to many users. Throughout this discussion, it has been shown that many users can neither identify the correct definitional differences between these methods nor distinguish between the two. The following discussion may aid in such necessary differentiation.

Spetzler classified the decision process into three basic steps: information gathering, calculation, and decision.[81] He then compared deterministic, probabilistic, and a certainty-equivalent method according to these steps. The importance of his work here is in his depiction of deterministic and probabilistic modeling and the role of sensitivity analysis.

With respect to the information-gathering step, both models are similar, although more information is required using risk analysis. Thus the amount of intangibles is reduced. The calculation step is more complex in risk analysis since stochasticity is entered, typically through a Monte Carlo process. But according to Spetzler, sensitivity analysis forms an integral part of the deterministic model. In other words, prior to entering the decision state, sensitivities must be examined in order to have the necessary information to make an effective review, and thus a decision. Therefore, sensitivity analysis becomes a crucial factor in investment analysis.

The point is not that probabilistic modeling cannot use sensitivity analysis. Pyhrr and others argued that it can and should be a part of a complete risk analysis. However, the implication from Spetzler is that it is an integral part of deterministic modeling, one which cannot be overlooked or briefly discarded.

Real estate investment analysis has failed to provide such a complete sensitivity analysis for the valuation model generally used. Until such an analysis can be done and its results integrated into the investment decision theory, real estate investment analysis will be lacking the information for effective decision analysis. This study may satisfy that need.

Summary

It has been shown that many developments applicable to real estate investment decision-making can be found in the literature of management science and operations research. However, few writers have made use of these developments. This has no doubt been one of the chief reasons for many of the misunderstandings that have been propagated in real estate investment analysis in recent works regarding the roles and concepts of models, techniques, and their applicability to real estate investment decision-making. The real estate literature has failed to distinguish between theories and models, models and real-world decision-making, simulation and modeling, or sensitivity analysis and simulation. This review has perhaps clarified these concepts and highlighted some of the distinctions between many of these tools.

This chapter has also introduced the reader to management science as a helpful discipline for real estate decision-making. This area has been surveyed along many lines such as the theory of models, the foundations of decision analysis, definitions of simulation, and the method of sensitivity analysis in management science. This chapter reviewed and highlighted some of the important developments in these areas to aid users in making real estate investment decisions.

Notes

1. James L. Riggs and Michael S. Inoue, *Introduction to Operations Research and Management Science: A General Systems Approach* (New York: McGraw-Hill Book Co., 1975), pp. 2-3.
2. R.E.D. Woolsey, "Operations Research and Management Science Today, or Does an Education in Checkers Really Prepare One for a Life of Chess?," *Operations Research* 20 (May-June 1972): 737.
3. Riggs and Inoue, *Operations Research,* p. 2.
4. Harney M. Wagner, *Principles of Operations Research,* 2d ed. (Englewood Cliffs, N.J.: Prenltice-Hall, 1975), pp. 5-6.
5. Ibid., p. 10.
6. John S. Hammond, "The Roles of the Manager and Management Scientist in Successful Implementation," *Sloan Management Review* 15 (Winter 1975): 9-11.
7. Herbert A. Simon, *The New Science of Management Decisions* (New York: Harper and Row, 1960), p. 1.
8. Robert Ferber and P.J. Verdoun, *Research Methods in Economics and Business* (New York: Macmillan Co., 1962), p. 30.
9. Russell L. Ackoff, "The Development of Operations Research as a Science," *Operations Research* 4 (June 1956): 265-266.
10. Thomas H. Naylor and Donald S. Burdick, "The Interface Between Simulation Experiments and Real World Experiments," in *A Survey of Statistical Design and Linear Models,* ed. by Jagish N. Srivastava (Amsterdam: North-Holland Publishing Co., 1975), p. 427. See also Thomas N. Naylor, Joseph L. Balinty, Donald S. Burdick, and King Chu, *Computer Simulation Techniques* (New York: John Wiley and Sons, 1966), pp. 23-42.
11. Naylor and Burdick, "Simulation Experiments," pp. 429-430.
12. Riggs and Inoue, *Operations Research,* p. 8.
13. E. Frank Harrison, *The Managerial Decision-Making Process* (Boston: Houghton Mifflin Co., 1975), p. 41.
14. Daniel Teichroew, *An Introduction to Management Science—Deterministic Models* (New York: John Wiley and Sons, 1965), p. 3.
15. Arne Mjosund, "The Synergy of Operations Research and Computers," *Operations Research* 20 (September-October 1972): 1057.
16. Herbert A. Simon and Allen Newell, "Heuristic Problem Solving: The Next Advance in Operations Research," *Operations Research* 6 (January-

February 1958): 3. See also Giuseppe M. Ferrero di Roccaferrera, *Operations Research Models for Business and Industry* (Cincinnati, Ohio: South-Western Publishing Co., 1964), p. 20.

17. John P. Crecine, *Governmental Problem-Solving* (Chicago: Rand McNally and Co., 1969), p. 23.

18. Robert R. Singleton and William F. Tyndall, *Games and Programs: Mathematics for Modeling* (San Francisco: W.H. Freeman and Co., 1974), p. xvi. For descriptions of types of models, see Paul H. Rigby, *Models in Business Analysis* (Columbus, Ohio: Charles E. Merrill Publishing Co., 1969), pp. 4-8; Geoffrey Gordon, *System Simulation* (Englewood Cliffs, N.J.: Prentice-Hall, 1969), pp. 7, 12; Robert J. Thierauf and Robert C. Klekamp, *Decision Making Through Operations Research,* 2d ed. (New York: John Wiley and Sons, 1975), pp. 17-19.

19. Robert Durbin, *Theory Building* (New York: Free Press, 1969), p. 14.

20. William J. Baumol, "Economic Models and Mathematics," in *The Structure of Economic Science,* ed. by Sherman Roy Krupp (Englewood Cliffs, N.J.: Prentice-Hall, 1961), pp. 88-101.

21. Rigby, *Models in Business Analysis,* p. 32.

22. Naylor, Balinty, Burdick, and Chu, *Computer Simulation Techniques,* p. 9.

23. Ira Horowitz, *Introduction to Quantitative Business Analysis* (New York: McGraw-Hill Book Co., 1972), pp. 6-7.

24. L.R. Carter and E. Hazan, *A Practical Approach to Computer Simulation in Business* (New York: John Wiley and Sons, 1973), p. 25.

25. Wagner, *Operations Research,* p. 10.

26. John C.G. Boot, *Mathematical Reasoning in Economics and Management Science* (Englewood Cliffs, N.J.: Prentice-Hall, 1967), p. 126.

27. Gordon, *System Simulation,* p. 5.

28. Irwin D.J. Bross, "Models," in *Management Systems,* ed. by Peter Schoderbek, 2d ed. (New York: John Wiley and Sons, 1971), pp. 146-147.

29. G. Anthony Gorry, "The Development of Managerial Models," *Sloan Management Review* 12 (Winter 1971): 3.

30. J.D. Little, "Models and Managers: The Concept of a Decision Calculus," *Management Science* 16 (April 1970): B-467.

31. James R. Emshoff and Roger L. Sisson, *Decision and Use of Computer Simulation Models* (New York: Macmillan Co., 1970), p. 50.

32. Herbert A. Simon, *Administrative Behavior,* 2d ed. (New York: Free Press, 1965), p. 142.

33. D.N. Chorafas, *Systems and Simulation* (New York: Academic Press, 1965), p. 31.

34. Harold Bierman, Charles P. Bonini, and Warren H. Hausman, *Quantitative Analysis for Business Decisions,* 4th ed. (Homewood, Ill.: Richard D. Irwin, 1973), p. 3.

35. Ibid.

36. Robert O. Schlaifer, *Analysis of Decisions under Uncertainty* (New York: McGraw-Hill Book Co., 1969), p. 65.

37. Federick S. Hillier and Gerald J. Lieberman, *Introduction to Operations Research* (San Francisco: Holden-Day, 1967), p. 444.

38. Chester R. Wasson, *Understanding Quantitative Analysis* (New York: Appleton-Century-Crofts, 1969), p. 2.

39. D. Warner North, "A Tutorial Introduction to Decision Theory," *IEEE Transactions on Systems Science and Cybernetics* SCC–4 (September 1968): 210.

40. Ronald A. Howard, "Decision Analysis: Applied Decision Theory," *Proceedings of the Fourth International Conference on Operational Research* (August 29-September 2, 1966): 71.

41. Johan von Neumann and Oscar Morgenstern, *Theory of Games and Economic Behavior,* 2d ed. (Princeton, N.J.: Princeton University Press, 1947).

42. J.W. Pratt, Howard Raiffa, and Robert O. Schlaifer, "The Foundations of Decisions Under Uncertainty: An Elementary Exposition," *Journal of the American Statistical Association* 59 (1964): 353-375.

43. Ward Edwards, "The Theory of Decision Making," *Psychological Bulletin* 51 (July 1954), reprinted as chapter 33 in *Some Theories of Organization,* ed. by Albert H. Rubenstein and Chadwick J. Haverstrob (Homewood, Ill.: Richard D. Irwin, 1960), pp. 385-430.

44. For example, see R.D. Luce and Howard Raiffa, *Games and Decisions: Introduction and Critical Survey* (New York: John Wiley and Sons, 1957), chapter 2; Jack Clark Francis and Stephen A. Archer, *Portfolio Analysis* (Englewood Cliffs, N.J.: Prentice-Hall, 1971), pp. 197-201; William J. Baumol, *Economic Theory and Operations Analysis,* 2d ed. (Englewood Cliffs, N.J.: Prentice-Hall, 1972), pp. 536-552; Brian E. Forst, "Decision Analysis and Medical Malpractice," *Operations Research* 22 (January-February 1974): 1-12.

45. Ronald A. Howard, "The Foundations of Decision Analysis," *IEEE Transactions on Systems Science and Cybernetics* SSC–4 (September 1968): 211-219.

46. Howard, "Decision Analysis," p. 155.

47. Howard, "Decision Analysis," p. 215.

48. Samuel Eilon, "What Is a Decision?," *Management Science* 16 (December 1969): B-172-174.

49. Howard, "Decision Analysis," p. 55.

50. Howard Raiffa, *Decision Analysis–Introductory Lectures in Choices Under Uncertainty* (Menlo Park, Calif.: Addison Wesley, 1968), pp. 270-272.

51. D.J. White, *Decision Methodology* (New York: John Wiley and Sons, 1975), pp. 42, 56.

52. Ibid., p. 63.

53. Luce and Raiffa, *Games and Decisions,* p. 13.

54. Samuel B. Richmond, *Operations Research for Management Decisions* (New York: Ronald Press Co., 1968), p. 31.

55. Ronald J. Ebert and Terence R. Mitchell, *Organizational Decision Processes* (New York: Crane, Russak and Company, 1975), p. 45.

56. Kenneth J. Arrow, "Decision Theory and Operations Research," *Operations Research* 5 (December 1957): 765.

57. G.T. Jones, *Simulation and Business Decisions* (Middlesex, England: Penguin Books, 1972), p. 98.

58. Joe H. Mize and J. Grady Cox, *Essentials of Simulation* (Englewood Cliffs, N.J.: Prentice-Hall, 1968), p. 1.

59. Patric Rivett, *Principles of Model Building* (London: John Wiley and Sons, 1972), p. 109.

60. Ibid., p. 115.

61. Naylor, Balinty, Burdick, and Chu, *Computer Simulation Techniques*, p. 1.

62. K.D. Tocher, "The State of the Art of Simulation—A Survey," *Proceedings of the Fourth International Conference on Operational Research* (August 29-September 2, 1966): 693-701.

63. Daniel Teichroew and John Francis Lubin, "Computer Simulation—Discussion of the Technique and Comparison of Languages," *Communications of the ACM* 9 (October 1966): 724.

64. Thomas H. Naylor, "Computer Simulation: A Managerial Decision Tool," *Papers and Case Histories of the Twenty-Fourth International Systems Meeting* (April 18-21, 1971): p. 77.

65. Jones, *Simulation*, p. 98.

66. George K. Chacko, *Computer-Aided Decision-Making* (New York: American Elsevier Publishing Co., 1972), p. 291. See also Naylor, "Computer Simulation," p. 78; and Claude McMillan and Richard F. Gonzalez, *Systems Analysis*, 3d ed. (Homewood, Ill.: Richard D. Irwin, 1973), p. 17.

67. Rigby, *Models in Business Analysis*, p. 12.

68. Mize and Cox, *Essentials of Simulation*, pp. 1, 186.

69. James C.T. Mao, *Quantitative Analysis of Financial Decisions* (New York: Macmillan Co., 1969), p. 554.

70. Thomas H. Naylor, Donald S. Burdick, and W. Earl Sasser, Jr., "The Design of Computer Simulation Experiments," in *The Design of Computer Simulation Experiments*, ed. by Thomas H. Naylor (Durham, N.C.: Duke University Press, 1969), p. 4. See also Naylor, Balinty, Burdick, and Chu, *Computer Simulation Techniques*, p. 3; Naylor, "Computer Simulation," p. 76; and Robert C. Meier, William T. Newell, and Harold L. Payer, *Simulation in Business and Economics* (Englewood Cliffs, N.J.: Prentice-Hall, 1969), p. 2.

71. C. West Churchman, "An Analysis of the Concept of Simulation," in *Symposium on Simulation Models*, ed. by Austin C. Hoggatt and Frederick E. Balderstrom (Cincinnati, Ohio: South-Western Publishing Co., 1963), p. 12.

72. Thomas H. Naylor, Donald S. Burdick, and W. Earl Sasser, "Computer Simulation Experiments with Economic Systems: The Problem of Experimental Design," *Journal of the American Statistical Association* 62 (December 1967): 1316. See also P.R. Williams and D.L. Weeks, "A Technique for Designing and Augmenting Simulation Experiments," *Management Science* 20 (1974): 1385-1392; J.S. Hunter and T.H. Naylor, "Experimental Design for Computer Simulation Experiments," *Management Science* 16 (March 1970): 422–434.

73. Aaron Fleisher, "The Uses of Simulation," in *Computer Methods in the Analysis of Large-Scale Social Systems,* ed. by James M. Beshers, 2d ed. (Cambridge, Mass.: MIT Press, 1968), p. 189.

74. Richard E. Dawson, "Simulation in the Social Sciences," in *Simulation in Social Science: Readings,* ed. by Harold S. Guetzkow (Englewood Cliffs, N.J.: Prentice-Hall, 1962), p. 3. See also John Harling, "Simulation Techniques in Operations Research–A Review," *Operations Research* 6 (May-June 1958): 307-319; Carter and Hazan, *Computer Simulation,* pp. 13-14; Richard F. Barton, *A Primer on Simulation and Gaming* (Englewood Cliffs, N.J.: Prentice-Hall, 1970), pp. 7, 19; and Stephen Paranka, *Business Applications of Decision Sciences* (New York: Petrocelli/Charter Publishers, 1975), p. 89.

75. Victor B. Godin, "The Dollars and Sense of Simulation," *Decision Sciences* 7 (April 1976): 331-342.

76. J. Harry Goldie, "Simulation and Irritation," in *Corporate Simulation Models,* ed. by Albert N. Schreiber (Seattle, Wash.: University of Washington Printing Plant, 1970), pp. 614-646.

77. Richard L. Van Horn, "Validation of Simulation Results," *Management Science* 17 (January 1971): 251.

78. William Bentz, Lawrence Sherr, and Robert Miller, "Sensitivity Analysis with Interaction Effects," *Decision Sciences* 7 (July 1976): 432.

79. Richard B. Maffei, "Simulation, Sensitivity and Management Decision Rules," *Journal of Business* 31 (July 1958): 186.

80. Baumol, *Operations Research,* p. 453.

81. Carl S. Spetzler, "The Development of a Corporate Risk Policy for Capital Investment Decisions," *IEEE Transactions on Systems Science and Cybernetics* SSC-4 (September 1968): 279.

3 Review of Sensitivity Studies in Real Estate Investment

There are a number of studies of rates of return in real estate investment. Some measured returns historically, or *ex post,* but most used expected discounted cash flow data, or *ex ante* models. A brief review is presented in this chapter but the reader is referred elsewhere for more extensive analysis.

The main purpose of this chapter is to review the many studies of the sensitivity of returns and values to changes in certain variables. It begins with some background material and a discussion of the relevance of sensitivity analysis for real estate investment studies. The discussion examines the relationship between sensitivity analysis, probabilistic modeling, and simulation. The chapter concludes with a review and summary of the major sensitivity studies. Some thirteen authors have studied various variables in the past few years and each of the major studies is reviewed and analyzed.

Studies of Real Estate Rates of Return

In 1972, Pyhrr suggested that only a "few scholarly studies of rates of return in multi-family rental housing have appeared in the literature."[1] He reviewed the major studies and highlighted the important differences between the studies and the conclusions and implications of each study.

The review presented here briefly highlights many of the same studies found in Pyhrr and updates with recent developments. Grebler's study of long-term investment found returns in real estate more volatile and variable than bonds or mortgages.[2] He concluded that returns to real estate were not as glamourous as one might expect when considering the risks associated with investments in real estate.[3] He found yields ranged from 0.94 percent for elevator apartments to 5.04 percent for walkup apartments. The data was for New York property but was very small in size (generally fewer than ten apartments per type).

Wendt and Wong (later Wendt and Tully) examined real estate returns in comparison to common stock returns. The former study used Federal Housing Administration (FHA) data for apartment houses and concluded that "10.8 percent of the average yield of 10.9 percent was due to tax shelter."[4] They suggested that "after-tax returns are the most significant criteria for evaluating portfolio decisions,"[5] and thus the after-tax return on equity appears as the most significant contribution of this paper and the basis for Wendt and Cerf's text in 1969.

Ricks studied hypothetical investment returns for insurance company multifamily data with mortgages of $100,000 and higher.[6] He listed nine input assumptions for use with this discounted cash flow planning model and on the basis of these assumptions presented results for rates of return to equity, before and after taxation and financing.[7] The results indicated that returns varied between 7.5 and 12.4 percent on a before-tax basis and between 4.7 and 9.6 percent after taxes have been paid, for the periods studied. His study demonstrated the effect of leverage on property and since the returns were ex ante (that is, not based on actual data but on expected future returns), Ricks argued that models of this type are useful for investment planning.

Soelberg and Stefaniak analyzed ex ante IRRs in attempting to assess the economic impact of the 1969 Tax Reform Bill on real estate investments. By varying depreciation, tax rates, and debt to equity ratios, they derived returns to equity varying from 4.05 to 13.46 percent.[8] An unusual set of justifications was established to enable property cost to equal property value over time. These included the appropriate combination of expected price changes, an average estimate of neighborhood deterioration, increased population growth, and increasing obsolescence of the property.[9]

Sunley compared his results with those of Soelberg and Stefaniak.[10] By varying depreciation and recapture rules for two levels of equity and tax rates, he concluded, among other things, that the impact of the Tax Reform Act did not affect rates of return as much as many investors had feared. He suggested that the "effect of changes in depreciation and recapture are about equivalent to the effect of a one percentage point increase in mortgage interest rates."[11] His results varied from 11.2 to 25.4 percent returns on equity before the Tax Reform Act and 10.3 to 25.4 percent after the Act. He suggested that the major differences between his model and that of Soelberg and Stefaniak were the results of underlying assumptions, principally the level of net operating income.[12]

Davis' study found only 7 percent average returns to equity.[13] This finding suggested his hypothesis was correct in that management must be an important factor since returns are relatively low. He observed that management makes the difference.[14] Davis suggested that "leverage, depreciation and capital gains are key influences determining rates of return."[15] But he found that the quality rather than the quantity of management is the crucial factor.

Roulac recently surveyed many of these and other studies in an attempt to compare real estate and common stock returns as originally proposed by Wendt and Wong.[16] He chiefly examined the methodology and results of most historical studies but also treated issues such as risk, market efficiency, the influence of management, multitiered markets, and expectations of return. He concluded that the lack of empirical evidence precluded conclusions as to the superiority of real estate over common stocks as investments. However, he suggested that real estate is less variable and thus less risky than common stocks. He also observed that the real estate markets are less efficient than capital markets. Since information was more valuable for real estate decision makers, management could exert more influence over returns than could investors in common stock.[17]

Background and Assumptions of Sensitivity Studies

Sensitivity analysis is a technique which has been used or advocated by many real estate authors. Hysom and Juengling,[18] Wendt,[19] Pyhrr,[20] Cooper and Morrison,[21] Blazar and Hilton,[22] Maisel and Roulac,[23] Beaton and Robertson,[24] and others urged use of this technique but generally failed to provide any results. A few authors suggested the importance of certain variables without any sensitivity results. McNeeley, for example, stated that the key items include cash investment, rental income, operating expenses, vacancy, expenses, interest, and principal repayments.[25] Recht and Loewenstein argued for a more careful and analytical approach and urged analysts to seek more objective and current information about variations in rates of return.[26] It is the contention of the current study that this development has not taken place, despite several sensitivity studies and much interest in this area. A review of these studies follows and demonstrates the inadequacies of the results.

The Relevance of Sensitivity Analysis for Real Estate Investment

Thorne pointed out the importance of this technique in analyzing real estate projects by emphasizing that these variables called critical will determine the feasibility of projects and that changes in these must be isolated to evaluate the effect on the bottom line.[27]

Dasso, Kinnard, and Messner suggested that sensitivity analysis could be used to answer either of two questions: what is necessary to achieve a yield, and what is the impact on yield of a change in assumption.[28] Messner, Schreiber, and Lyon envisioned sensitivity analysis as a practical tool for analysts which enabled the analysis of the sensitivity of value or return as a result of changes in elements of the cash flow.[29]

In reference to sensitivity analysis and probabilistic analysis, Thorne pointed out the often misunderstood relationship and limitations of sensitivity analysis. However, he warned that risk simulation may not recognize some of the dependent relationships that sensitivity analysis would pick up.[30]

Although Pyhrr has traditionally argued that deterministic sensitivity analysis and probabilistic risk analysis are separate techniques, he stated that sensitivity analysis is possible and valuable within the risk analysis model.[31] Others suggested that the relationship between sensitivity analysis and simulation is very close. Horowitz stated that sensitivity analysis seeks to analyze whether an assumption really makes any difference with respect to output.[32] Robichek and Myers stated that simulation "refers to the systematic projection of results under alternative assumptions" and "a common sense approach to the evaluation of uncertainty [is] to rerun the simulation using revised sets of assumptions in the mode," (that is, perform sensitivity analysis).[33] Wendt and Tandy implied there was no difference between deterministic modeling and simulation since "using the techniques of computer simulation" (i.e., the computerization of PCF models) can assist the analyst in exploring the assumptions on value or return.[34] But in the following paragraphs, they implied that sensitivity analysis was a distinct analytic technique and with simulation, these qualified as examples of heuristic decision-making. While it is highly questionable whether sensitivity analysis and simulation are interchangeable concepts, it is even more questionable as to whether sensitivity analysis is heuristic because it involves "the use of trial-and-error techniques rather than routine, computational algorithms for problem solving."[35]

Sensitivity Studies

To facilitate comparisons of the studies, each is briefly reviewed and summarized according to (1) variables examined, (2) results obtained, and (3) conclusions and implications reached. The final sections present a comparative analysis of the findings of all the studies and a summary concludes the chapter.

The Shenkel Studies (1969)

While the purpose of these two articles was not the same as that found in most of the studies included here, these studies are relevant since both emphasize certain variables as being important in valuation. In the first study, Shenkel examined the importance of many variables using the Ellwood technique.[36] He concluded that the loan to value ratio, the mortgage interest rate, and the mortgage term were significant variables, in that order. He also found that the holding period was less important in terms of its impact on yield and that appreciation or depreciation over the holding period would substantially affect value.[37]

In the second study, Shenkel examined various land/building ratios and the effects of different depreciation methods.[38] While he did not examine other variables, the implication was that these are the variables that are most important in terms of affecting return and value. Since both studies are primarily for demonstration purposes, Shenkel was unconcerned about overlooking other important variables.

The Higgins and Cunningham Study (1970)

It is well known now that this study contains two conceptual errors prior to the discussion of sensitivity analysis. The first error was their adoption of the rate of return on total capital rather than the return on equity.[39] They selected this measure since they felt that the return on total capital was a better measure of productivity.

The second error was in their adoption of the use of sensitivity analysis to measure risk. They suggested that sensitivity analysis "entails noting the magnitude by which the expected return . . . changes as we change our estimates of prospective cash flows—the larger the magnitude of the change in the expected return, the larger the risk."[40] They advocated the use of sensitivity analysis to examine four variables: future rental rates, occupancy rates, expenses, and sales prices. However, they did not provide results of any analysis.

The Sunley Study (1970)

As discussed earlier, this study examined the effects of depreciation and recapture rules which resulted from changes according to the Tax Reform Act of 1969. Sunley examined changes in four variables; pre-1969 and post-1969 depreciation and recapture tax provisions, marginal income tax of the investor, equity ratio, and the type of real estate.[41]

His results indicated that a change in depreciation from 200 to 150 percent declining balance, or from 150 percent declining balance to straight-line depreciation, is relatively more important than changes in recapture. He also found that changes in depreciation and recapture were more important for investors in the 70 percent tax bracket than for those in the 50 percent bracket. He found that investors in a 70 percent tax bracket made a better after-tax return than those in the 50 percent bracket, indicating the difficulty of using depreciation as an economic incentive. He also discovered that returns were substantially higher for investments when equity was at 10 percent of the total rather than at 20 percent (or higher) as a result of leverage.[42]

The importance of this study for sensitivity analysis is not as clear. By implication, Sunley suggested that changes in depreciation, tax rates, percentage of equity (or loan to value ratio), and possibly recapture provisions are important influences on return. While he did not examine which was most important, it would be fair to assume that his emphasis on these variables suggests he has assumed changes in these variables would be significantly important.

The Ricks Study (1971)

A less well-known study by Ricks examined the sensitivity of return to changes in three variables: growth in reversion, holding period, and down payment.[43] He demonstrated the effect on rate of return of changes in holding period from five to ten years, varying the growth in reversion from 0 to 3 percent compounded annually, and testing the effect of leverage by varying down payments from 10 to 20 percent. In considering the combined effects of leverage and appreciation, this resulted in raising after-tax return on equity from 4.3 to 15.7 percent.[44] He also suggested the further altering of assumptions to "conduct an appraisal of the property's worth to [the investor]."[45] While the altering of input assumptions technically constitutes sensitivity analysis, Ricks's paper is merely one demonstration of possible impacts on return altering only three variables.

The Gallagher Study (1971)

This is one of the more important and interesting of the sensitivity studies. Based upon a typical investment property from the 1968 Annual Apartment Building Income-Expense Analysis publication of the Institute of Real Estate Management, Gallagher incorporated many ideas into his study.[46] First, his method of a typical case property has been adopted by many studies, including this one. Second, he examined changes in six significant parameters: the investor's tax rate, cost, loan to value ratio, mortgage interest rate, property growth rate, and the depreciation method.[47] Third, he advocated the use of the high-base-low approach for the sensitivity analysis. Finally, although this framework permitted only three changes on each variable, Gallagher argued that those changes ought to be determined based upon some weighting scheme. He used subjective limits that a typical investor might consider for various parameters. In effect, Gallagher provided justification for the arbitrariness of his upper and lower limits by attempting to explain away this problem.

This is the only justification for such modifications, in that Gallagher proceeded to specify the low, base, and high inputs for the six parameters he examined. This author is aware of the problem Gallagher tried to treat and hopes to handle it better by using empirical data in chapter 5.

Gallagher used the following input parameter values in his study. For the investor's tax rate, he used 20 percent, 35 percent, and 50 percent; for the cost of the project, $396,000, $440,000, and $484,000; for the loan to value ratio,

60 percent, 75 percent, and 90 percent; for the mortgage rate, 6 percent, 8 percent, and 10 percent. He allowed the annual property growth rate to vary from 0 to 2 to 4 percent, and the depreciation method from straight line to 125 percent declining balance to 150 percent declining balance.

He provided explanations for each of these changes. The ranges were assumed to cover the upper and lower limits of the typical investor's utility preference scale. This, he suggested, was the justification for 15 percent changes on the loan to value ratio base of 75 percent, and 15 percent changes from a 35 percent tax rate base.[48] On a percentage basis, these changes are not the same (20 and 42.86 percent, respectively). For the mortgage interest rate and the yearly growth rate, each was changed two percentage points on each side of the base rate of 8 and 2 percent, respectively. However, on a percentage basis, these rates were varied 25 and 100 percent, respectively.[49] Thus, the real percentage changes were thought to be more helpful in testing sensitivities than equal percentage point changes as others have done.

Gallagher's results indicated that the four most important variables were the loan to value ratio, appreciation in value, interest rate, and cost, in that order. The tax rate and depreciation method used were found to be relatively unimportant.[50] Gallagher also presented conflicting results for a one-year holding period investment, given the other results. If the investor were to sell after one year, the loan to value ratio becomes unimportant and the depreciation method increases in significance.[51] The implicit variable to be examined is the relevance of the holding period. Gallagher omitted this analysis.

The Walters Studies (1971-73)

Walters, a leader in the area of computerization and investment analysis, reported three studies during the period 1971-73. The first two are of less importance than the third, which formed the basis for this thesis. Walters demonstrated the "application of computerized capitalization rate routines to appraisal sensitivity analysis."[52] This was a method that appraisers could use to "determine how a project's value changes as each of several valuation factors are varied."[53]

He chose six variables: rate of appreciation, mortgage term, holding period, loan to value ratio, interest rate on debt, and required equity yield. For these parameters, he demonstrated a variety of changes; for appreciation, from -20 to +20 percent; for the mortgage term, from fifteen to thirty-five years; and for the holding period, from five to seventeen years. He also varied the loan to value ratio from 60 to 80 percent; the mortgage interest rate from 6 to 10 percent, and the required equity yield from 10 to 26 percent over eight changes.

It is interesting to note that a priori Walters implied that of the six variables he thought were significant, three were considered to be more significant than the others. One of these, the length of the holding period, turns out to have practically no effect in his *Journal of Property Management* paper. The approach in this paper was the use of income multipliers and sensitivity charts. He suggested this before-tax measure since it avoided problems with taxation, depreciation, and capital gains.[54]

His results indicated that the effect of interest rate changes on value "lose their importance as the investor's required equity yield increases." However, for the loan to value ratio, the opposite effect occurs. As the initial yield increases, the loan to value ratio increases in importance. He found the mortgage term to be very insignificant. However, his holding period results were more complicated. He concluded that changes in the holding period are insignificant when coupled with no growth but very important when the terminal value or revision increases or declines.[55] Therefore, for the appraiser, Walters suggested this finding would be significant. Since the importance of the project's holding period changes dramatically with the growth assumption, the importance of dequate market analysis cannot be overlooked, Walters argued.

The second study presented justifications of the importance of sensitivity analysis for appraisers. For example, he argued that with this knowledge the appraiser could more efficiently use his time and resources in devoting his attention to important variables.[56] Thus, as Whisler also argued throughout his work, one can view sensitivity analysis as a process of determining the impact of errors on the estimates of value or return.

In this study, Walters selected seven variables for analysis: the same six as in the previous study plus net income. He tested each of these variables for positive and negative 10 percent changes rather than numerical changes. While his results were relatively inconclusive, he found the holding period to be relatively unimportant. The analyst would be able to provide a better overall analysis by devoting more time to estimating variables such as net income or desired yield on equity than on determining the optimum holding period.[57]

Walters' third and most important study formed the basis of the "Importance of property management" hypothesis. In this study Walters combined sections of both previous studies for this larger and more complete work.[58] He selected thirteen variables and presented results for a typical project, given favorable 10 percent changes in each variable. Thus, if an increase in the variable would increase yield (IRR), this would mean a 10 percent increase in the variable would be favorable. If decreasing a variable such as cost would mean an increase in yield, this would mean a 10 percent decrease in the variable would be favorable. The results would show increase in yield as a result of all changes.

Walters warned that "since the purpose of this article is only to demonstrate the relative importance of the various factors, some digression from the realities of the investment world can be ignored."[59] Thus he observed what the effect of 137 percent declining balance depreciation would have, although regulations may not allow such a rate. Similar justification could be found for other unrealistic impacts.

His results are very dramatic and clear (see table 3-1). He observed that

Table 3-1
Results of Walters' "Importance of Property Management" Study

Variable Group and Variable	*Impact on Yield Percent*	*Ranking of Importance*
Property management		
Gross income	30.3	1
Operating expenses	11.9	4
Fiscal, monetary, and housing policy		
Interest on mortgage	12.7	3
Mortgage financing	11.8	5
Mortgage term	2.6	8
Purchase and sale		
Cost	20.3	2
Selling expenses	5.0	6.5
Property value growth rate	5.0	6.5
Taxation		
Allowable depreciation method	2.2	9
Owner's tax bracket	1.6	10
Depreciable basis	1.1	11
Depreciable life	1.0	12
Holding period	.5	13

Source: David W. Walters, "Just How Important Is Property Management?" *Journal of Property Management* (Chicago: Institute of Real Estate Management, vol. 38, July/August 1973), pp. 164, 168. Copyrighted. Reprinted with permission.

five of the variables have a substantially greater impact on yield than do the other eight. These are gross income, cost, interest rates, operating expenses, and mortgage financing.[60] He concluded by citing a number of findings:

1. The most important variable is the project's gross income. Property managers have long known the importance of good rental performance.

2. The second most important influence is the cost of acquiring the project at the right cost. But property management plays an important role in acquisition of property as well.

3. The third and fifth most important variables are interest and available mortgage financing and these are outside the control of the investor. However, Walters suggested good management is necessary to make up for interest rate policies.

4. The fourth variable is operating expenses, a variable under the control of the property manager.

5. The sixth variable is property value growth rate, an important concern but one that Walters feels, in light of this evidence, has been overstated. While "good economic forecasts are important in real estate decisions, attention to management variables cannot be forgotten."

6. Efficient management might be able to increase returns comparable to capital gains or potentially wasted selling expenses from an unnecessary sale.

7. The remaining variables (mortgage term, allowable depreciation method,

owner's tax bracket, depreciable basis, depreciable life, and holding period) have relatively little impact on yield. "Indeed, a 10 percent change in all of the remaining variables combined has less impact than a 10 percent change in the project's operating expenses."

8. Since most of the unimportant variables are associated with income taxation, one ought not think taxes are unimportant factors in real estate decision-making. What is unimportant is a change in any of these variables compared to a change in other variables.

9. Therefore, one ought to reconsider the role of property management in the investment decision. "It may very well be that a dollar spent for property management services can increase an investment's yield far beyond that of a dollar spent for tax advice."

10. When grouped into categories (as in table 3-1), "a change in the two variables associated with property management has about as much impact as a change in all of the other variables combined." Thus, a property manager can affect the return more than anyone else.

11. Therefore, the role of the property manager is as important as that of the tax consultant or economist. "The property manager may be the single most important decision-maker in the real estate investment process."[61]

Therefore, Walters' importance of property management hypothesis is a firm challenge to the profession. If his evidence is supported, one ought to reexamine the role of property management in the investment decision. If there are problems with the method of analysis, data, or other factors, one ought to know what they are. This study intends to directly provide answers to these challenges.

Gross has defined property management as "the branch of real estate composed of renting, supervising, collecting, paying, and the overall maintaining and managing of real estate for others."[62] While historically this profession has been thought to be merely rent collectors and thus relatively unimportant, this work may bring forth a reexamination of its role and importance in investment decision-making. The implication is that property management should take its place among such professions as tax accountancy, credit analysis and banking, and real estate appraising. Walters has suggested that it may even be foremost among these professions.

The Erler Study (1972)

This is an incomplete study of rates of return for income property using a simple computer model to derive results. Erler described the purpose of the paper as "a simple paradigm whereby an income property may be quickly analyzed for rate of return given . . . operating costs financial leverage, price and loan terms."[63] He then suggested that with such a model, sensitivity analysis could easily be performed.

Although no results were presented, there are two problems with this study. First, his use of gross income multipliers has been shown to be deficient in an earlier Walters' study, but here the multiplier tends to minimize changes in operating expenses. This leads to the second problem: as a result of the use of the multiplier, Erler's study appears to be misdirected in terms of importance of variables in the decision-making process. It is therefore easy to arrive at the conclusion he reached: although management may affect the operating expense ratio somewhat, it is an inherent characteristic of the property. The model focuses on the negotiable variables: price, down payment, interest rate, and loan terms.[64]

The Sprague Study (1973)

This short study presents examples of the impact of changes in three pro forma statement items on return: rental rates, occupancy rates, and operating expenses. Sprague noted the importance of this technique in that analysis of a pro forma statement may be much more enlightening after the results of a sensitivity analysis are available.[65] Sprague demonstrated three sets of changes; he varied initial rents of $255 per month from $235 to $275 per month. He produced changes in an initial return of 13.2 to 8.1 and 18.2 percent, respectively. He was able to observe that "a change of less than 4% in estimated average rent of $255 will produce a change of more than 19% in net operating income before taxes."[66]

Sprague also examined changes in occupancy rates from 91 to 99 percent. Returns varied from 10.4 to 15.9 percent as a result of the occupancy changes, assuming rents and responses in the initial case. Thus he observed a two percentage point change in the occupancy rate resulted in a loss of 10.3 percent net income, or a decrease of 1.4 percent in the equity return.[67] He then examined the effect of changes in operating expenses from $180,000 to $220,000. Based upon the initial values of the other parameters, rates of return varied from 15.4 to 10.9 percent. He thus observed that for each 5 percent increase in expenses, the rate fell by 1.1 percent.[68]

While it seems Sprague is actually measuring percentage point changes and not percent changes as he says, he emphasized that the variables in question are "the proper subjects of market analysis" and the ones he thought were important for sensitivity testing.

The Cooper and Pyhrr Study (1973)

This is one of the important sensitivity studies in the literature. Based upon Pyhrr's dissertation, there are many results and findings. However, many results conflict with those of other studies and many findings caused inconsistencies for the authors, given their other work. After some discussion about the advantages of computerization and a suggestion that other models calculate value rather than perform rate of return analysis,"[69] they present six results of their sensitivity analyses.

1. The after-tax rate of return on equity (YIELD) is affected by mortgage financing terms, interest, depreciation, and holding period. The after-tax rate of return on total cost (ROR) is not affected by the amount of cost of financing, but is affected by holding period and to some extent depreciation method used. Thus, they suggested, "analysts stress equity yield as the primary rate of return indicator in real estate instead of ROR."

2. Equity yields rise with high leverage (that is, loan to value ratio is .90). They commented that the effect is greater when interest rates are low.

3. Higher yields are obtained with higher rates of depreciation. They suggested that depreciation benefits are more valuable when the debt ratio was high (that is, given a 6 percent interest rate and a ten-year holding period, yields increase from 16.4 to 20.2 percent with 90 percent mortgage financing and accelerated depreciation, compared to increase from 10.3 to 11.6 percent with 75 percent financing as one switched to double-declining depreciation.

4. In determining the optimum holding period, the YIELD criteria implied a short holding period. Using the ROR, a longer period is suggested.

5. With growth rates in rental income (3 percent per year), operating expense ratio (1.335 percent per year), and property value (2.5 percent per year), YIELD was 50 percent higher and ROR was 35 percent higher than without growth in those factors.

6. "The two most critical variables affecting an investor's yield in apartment house investments are changes in property value and changes in rental income over time."[70]

Thus, in light of their extensive analysis and as a result of their sixth finding, the work is somewhat confusing, especially since the authors' apparently disregard their own advice. "Time should not be wasted forecasting values of variables that do not significantly affect the ultimate investment outcome," they maintain.[71] In view of their own evidence as well as other studies that have identified the crucial variables in decision-making, is it possible that Cooper and Pyhrr have failed to heed their own words?

Therefore, while their paper demonstrates the effects on certain variables of changes in other variables, its conclusions as to the importance of various variables seem incomplete. With the exception of the sixth result, one would think that all variables are relatively important according to these results. If this is the intended result, we have learned little from Cooper and Pyhrr's study.

The Bleck Study (1973)

This study demonstrated the impact on IRR of changes in estimates of construction costs, occupancy, rents, and interest rates on available mortgages.[72] Bleck provided numerical results based upon initial values of $800,000 original cost, 95 percent occupancy, $300 per month rental schedule, and 8 percent interest on the mortgage. He found that IRR would fall to 8.25 percent if construction costs were underestimated by 15 percent. If occupancy fell to 80 percent, IRR would decline to 5.75 percent. If rents were to fall by 15 percent, IRR would fall to 6.125 percent. If the mortgage rate were to increase to 8.75 percent, IRR would fall only to 12.50 percent.[73] Thus, he observed the impact of changes in occupancy and rent are severest, the impact of changes in cost estimates are of greater magnitude than the impact of changes in mortgage rates, which are relatively modest. Bleck provided no further conclusions but implied that rents and occupancy were more important than costs or mortgage rates.

The Hemmer Study (1975)

This study also stemmed from an earlier dissertation,[74] and was not a sensitivity analysis per se. It is generally a demonstration of the use of a discounted cash flow model and the benefits of computerization for real estate investors. Hemmer emphasized construction costs, growth rates, and residual values as the "three most important inputs to the economic valuation model."[75] This finding warranted this paper to be included in a review of sensitivity studies. Although the results are not shown and presumably were computed elsewhere, one can reasonably assume that Hemmer's choice of important variables relative to all others have been identified for the discounted cash flow model he proposed for use in his dissertation and he used in this study.

The Findlay and Howson Study (1975)

This differs from the previous studies in that rather than a discounted cash flow model, it uses dynamic programming to optimize valuation as a result of simultaneous changes in ownership, use, and valuation.[76] The sensitivity analysis is performed using this model with changes in three variables: return on equity, loan to value ratio, and interest rate. They found that value is substantially affected by changes in these variables. They suggested that the impact of credit availability and the spread between loan and equity rates had a "significant positive effect upon the value of the property."[77] In addition, they emphasized the importance of holding period considerations to maximize returns. While they failed to present evidence of the importance of holding period considerations, it is strongly implied to be a major concern.

The Whisler Study (1977)

A recent study by Whisler analyzed the impacts that errors (deviations from forecasts) can have in real estate investment analysis.[78] As implied earlier,

Table 3-2
Summary of Sensitivity Studies

	GI	*VAC*	*EGI*	*ΔGI*	*OE*	*NI*	*ΔOE*	*COUP*	*L/V*	*TERM*	*%DEP*	*DEPL*	*BAS*	*COST*	*ΔCOST*	*SE*	*TRATE*	*HP*	*R*
Shenkel (1969*a*)								+	+	+			+		+			–	
Shenkel (1969*b*)											+								
Higgins & Cunningham (1970)	+				+										+				
Sunley (1970)									+		+						+		
Ricks (1971)									+						+			+	
Gallagher (1971)								+	+		–			+	+		–	*	
Walters (1971)								+	+	–					+			*	+
Walters (1973*a*)						+		+	+	–					+			–	+
Walters (1973*b*)	+				+			+	+	–	–	–	–	+	–	–	–	–	–
Erler (1972)					–			+	+	+					+				
Sprague (1973)	+	+			+														
Cooper & Pyhrr (1973)	+			+			+	+	+	+	+				+			+	

Bleck (1973)	+	+				*		+			
Hemmer (1975)	-		+		+	-		+	+		
Findlay & Howson (1975)						+	+			+	+
Whisler (1977)		-		-	-	-	+		+		

Note: +(-) denotes study found or implied the variable to be significant (insignificant) in terms of impact on yield or values * denotes conflicting or inconclusive results; *GI* = gross income (rental rates); *VAC* = vacancy (1–occupancy); *EGI* = effective gross income; ΔGI = change in gross income growth rate; *OE* = operating expenses; *NI* = net operating income; ΔOE = change in operating expense growth rate; *COUP* = mortgage interest rate (interest rate on debt, interest rate, interest, interest on the mortgage); *L/V* = loan to value ratio (1–downpayment, 1–percent of equity, mortgage financing, a measure of financial leverage); *TERM* = mortgage term (loan term); *%DEP* = depreciation method; *DEPL* = depreciable life; *BAS* = depreciable basis (similar to land/building ratio); *COST* = property cost (construction costs); $\Delta COST$ = change in property cost (appreciation or depreciation over holding period, rate of appreciation, future selling price, price, reversion growth rate, property growth rate); *SE* = selling expenses; *TRATE* = effective income tax rate; *HP* = holding period; *R* = equity yield.

sensitivity analysis can be viewed as a tool to measure the costliness of errors due to imprecise estimates or forecasts. Whisler also developed the mathematical formulation elsewhere[79] and his work will be helpful in a later chapter in this study.

He examined the effect on yield of changes in estimates on seven variables. These included vacancy rates for three different periods, gas and electric expenses, future selling price, down payment, and mortgage interest rate. Through the use of an error factor, he reported the effects on rate of return. The value of his work, especially the *Journal of Finance* article, was in his mathematical derivation of this factor.

He pointed out that the results in his example were applicable only for this project; although using his methodology, the calculation of error factors is quite simple. Thus, he emphasized that the selling price was the most important variable he analyzed. The vacancies and gas and electric expenses were shown to have negligible effects on yield.

Similarly, Whisler's results suggested that sensitivity analysis can be helpful for investors when forecasting or estimating various inputs. He argued that the error factors could enable the investor or analyst to easily determine which estimates are critical, further enabling him to improve his decision-making abilities.[80]

A Comparative Analysis of Results

Table 3-2 presents a summary of the results of the sensitivity studies. It can easily be seen that a lack of consensus exists among the writers as to which variables' changes are most crucial in terms of their impact on yield. Most of the interest centers around a few variables: interest rate on the mortgage, loan to value ratio, and the future selling price (or growth in the reversion). The more controversial variables are gross income, mortgage term, depreciation method, tax rates, and holding period. One variable that has been generally overlooked is operating expenses.

Therefore, in light of the review and summary of the sensitivity studies, the importance of this work should be apparent. If the methodology and effort used in this thesis can objectively identify and measure the crucial impacts, this work should end some of the controversy and misunderstanding that has developed, as evidenced by the results found in table 3-2.

Summary

This chapter has identified some background studies in real estate and has extensively reviewed the studies that have either advocated, implied, or presented partial sensitivity analyses in real estate investment analysis. While a number of these studies have appeared, there seems to much uncertainty as to which variables are crucial in real estate decision-making. A careful analysis will show that for most variables, some writers believe changes in those variables would have a dramatic effect on yield or value, while others believe they would not. Similarly, other writers would suggest the importance of other variables over the initial ones selected. Some variables may have been overlooked by most writers.

This chapter has presented the results and findings presented by other writers. Perhaps this research may answer some of the questions which have been raised when attempting to reconcile differences in the studies.

Notes

1. Stephen A. Pyhrr, "A Proposed Model to Simulate Internal Rate of Return and Risk Characteristics of Investments in Multi-Family Rental Housing" (Ph.D. dissertation, University of Illinois at Urbana-Champaign, 1972), p. 87.

2. Leo Grebler, *Experience in Urban Real Estate Investment* (New York: Columbia University Press, 1955), p. 23.

3. Ibid., p. 25.

4. Paul F. Wendt and Sui N. Wong, "Investment Performance: Common Stocks Versus Apartment Houses," *Journal of Finance,* 20 (December 1965): 640. See also Paul F. Wendt and Gilbert Tully, "Investment Performance: Common Stocks Versus Apartment Houses," *The Appraisal Journal* 40 (January 1972): 123-127.

5. Wendt and Wong, "Investment Performance," p. 646.

6. R. Bruce Ricks, "Imputed Equity Returns on Real Estate Financed with Life Insurance Company Loans," *Journal of Finance* 24 (December 1969): 926-937.

7. Ibid., pp. 931-933.

8. Peer Soelberg and Norbert J. Stefaniak, "Impact of the Proposed Tax Reform Bill on Real Estate Investments," *The Appraisal Journal* 38 (April 1970): 188-211.

9. Ibid., p. 190.

10. Emil M. Sunley, Jr., "Changes in Depreciation and Recapture—Impact on Real Estate Investments," *The Appraisal Journal* 38 (October 1970): 524-535.

11. Ibid., p. 522.

12. Ibid., p. 533.

13. Irving F. Davis, *A Study of Real Estate Investment Returns to Capital and Management* (Fresno, Calif.: California State University Bureau of Business Research and Services, Study no. 14, July 1973), p. vii.

14. Ibid.

15. Ibid., p. 10.

16. Stephen E. Roulac, "Can Real Estate Returns Outperform Common Stocks?" *Journal of Portfolio Management* 2 (Winter 1976): 26–43.

17. Ibid., p. 38.

18. John Hysom and Charles Juengling, "Computerized Cash Flow Analysis," *Urban Land* 29 (October 1970): 162.

19. Paul F. Wendt, "Cash Flow Analysis by Computer," pp. 67–68.

20. Pyhrr, "A Proposed Model," p. 192.

21. James R. Cooper and Cathy A. Morrison, "Using Computer Simulation to Minimize Risk in Urban Housing Development," *The Real Estate Appraiser* 39 (March/April 1973): 17.

22. Sheldon Blazar and Hugh G. Hilton, "Investment Opportunities in Existing Apartment Buildings," *Real Estate Review* 6 (Summer 1976): 51.

23. Sherman J. Maisel and Stephen E. Roulac, *Real Estate Investment and Finance* (New York: McGraw-Hill Book Co., 1976), p. 410.

24. William R. Beaton and Terry Robertson, *Real Estate Investment,* 2d ed. (Englewood Cliffs, N.J.: Prentice Hall, 1977), p. 174.

25. W.S. McNeeley, "Money-Making in Real Estate Is a Numbers Game," *Real Estate Review* 2 (Spring 1972): 17.

26. J. Richard Recht and Louis K. Loewenstein, "Variations in Rates of Return," *The Appraisal Journal* 33 (April 1965): 248.

27. Oakleigh J. Thorne, "Real Estate Financial Analysis–The State of the Art," *The Appraisal Journal* 42 (January 1974): 36.

28. Jerome J. Dasso, William N. Kinnard, Jr., and Stephen D. Messner, "Lender Participation Financing: Applications of Sensitivity and Investment Analysis," *The Real Estate Appraiser* 37 (July/August 1971): 33–34.

29. Stephen D. Messner, Irving Schreiber, and Victor L. Lyon, *Marketing Investment Real Estate* (Chicago: Realtors National Marketing Institute of the National Association of Realtors, 1975) p. 264.

30. Thorne, "Real Estate Financial Analysis," p. 37.

31. Stephen A. Pyhrr, "Real Estate Risk Analysis Goes Scientific," *Real Estate Review* 2 (Fall 1973): 65; idem, "A Proposed Model," p. 218; David B. Hertz, "Risk Analysis in Capital Investment," *Harvard Business Review* 42 (January/February 1966): 105.

32. Ira Horowitz, *An Introduction to Quantitative Business Analysis,* 2d ed. (New York: McGraw-Hill Book Co., 1972), pp. 289–290.

33. Alexander A. Robichek and Stewart L. Myers, *Optimal Financing Decisions* (Englewood Cliffs, N.J.: Prentice-Hall, 1965), pp. 151–152.

34. Paul F. Wendt and Janet Tandy, "Evaluation of DCF Models in Real Estate Investment Analysis," rev. ed., April 1976 (mimeographed).

35. Ibid., p. 7.

36. William M. Shenkel, "Equity-Capitalization and Investment Decisions:

An Application of Conversational Computer Programming," *Journal of Property Management* 34 (March/April 1969): 76-87.

37. Ibid., pp. 84-85.

38. William M. Shenkel, "Cash Flow Analysis: An Application of Conversational Computer Programming," *Journal of Property Management* 34 (July/August 1969): 165-172.

39. Robert C. Higgins and R. Hugh Cunningham, "Computerized Calculations–Rate of Return and Risks in Commercial Property," *The Appraisal Journal* 38 (January 1970): 37-49.

40. Ibid., p. 41.

41. Sunley, "Changes in Depreciation and Recapture," pp. 524-535.

42. Ibid., pp. 527-531.

43. R. Bruce Ricks, "Computers and the Real Estate Investment Process" in Walters, ed., *Real Estate Computerization* (Berkeley, Calif.: Center for Real Estate and Urban Economics, Research Report, no. 35, 1971), pp. 154-160.

44. Ibid., p. 159.

45. Ibid.

46. Edward F. Gallagher, "Sensitivity Analysis for Apartment House Investment Property," in Walters, ed., *Real Estate Computerization,* p. 191.

47. Ibid., p. 192.

48. Ibid., p. 202.

49. Ibid.

50. Ibid., p. 226.

51. Ibid., p. 227.

52. David W. Walters, "Valuation Sensitivity Analysis," in Walters, ed., *Real Estate Computerization,* p. 55; also in *The Appraisal Journal* 41 (October 1973): 567-577.

53. Ibid.

54. Ibid., p. 65.

55. Ibid., p. 74.

56. David W. Walters, "Priorities in Appraisal Analysis," *Assessors Journal* 8 (October 1973): 4.

57. Ibid., p. 7.

58. David W. Walters, "Just How Important Is Property Management?" *Journal of Property Management* 38 (July/August 1973): 164-168.

59. Ibid., p. 165.

60. Ibid.

61. Ibid., pp. 165-168.

62. Jerome S. Gross, *Illustrated Encyclopedic Dictionary of Real Estate Terms* (Englewood Cliffs, N.J.: Prentice-Hall, 1969), p. 396.

63. Raymond L. Erler, "Rate of Return and Financial Leverage: A Paradigm for Sensitivity Analysis," *The Appraisal Journal* 40 (July 1972): 369.

64. Ibid., p. 377.

65. Willard F. Sprague, "Beware the Pro Forma, or How to Use Sensitivity Analysis," *Real Estate Review* 3 (Summer 1973): 114.

66. Ibid., p. 115.

67. Ibid.

68. Ibid., p. 116.

69. James R. Cooper and Stephen A. Pyhrr, "Forecasting the Rates of Return on an Apartment Investment: A Case Study," *The Appraisal Journal* 41 (July 1973): 315.

70. Ibid., pp. 327-334.

71. Ibid., p. 334.

72. Erick K. Bleck, "Real Estate Investments and Rates of Return," *The Appraisal Journal* 41 (October 1973): 543.

73. Ibid., pp. 543-546.

74. Edgar H. Hemmer, "A Valuation Model for Investments in Real Estate" (Ph.D. dissertation, Purdue University, 1972).

75. Edgar H. Hemmer, "How a Computer 'Thinks' About Real Estate," *Real Estate Review* 4 (Winter 1975): 119.

76. M. Chapman Findlay, III, and Hugh R. Howson, "Optimal Intertemporal Real Estate Ownership, Valuation, and Use," *American Real Estate and Urban Economics Journal* 3 (Summer 1975): 51.

77. Ibid., p. 65.

78. William D. Whisler, "Analyzing the Effects of Deviations from Forecasts in Real Estate Investment Analysis," *The Appraisal Journal* 45 (January 1977): 35–48.

79. William D. Whisler, "Sensitivity Analysis of Rates of Return," *Journal of Finance* 31 (March 1976): 63-69.

80. Whisler, "Effects of Deviations," p. 46.

4 Model Specification and Mathematical Sensitivity Analyses

Introduction

Chapter 4 is the core of this study. Having reviewed the various sensitivity studies in chapter 3, this chapter presents the equity valuation model for real estate investments. Although the general form of the model is well known, it is necessary to specify explicitly the precise functional relationships to permit examination of the crucial variables in the sensitivity analysis that follows.

Once the model has been specified, the technique of partial differentiation can be used to determine the changes that would occur in the function as a result of changes in the variable under study. The results would indicate the magnitude and direction of the change, and thus would aid in identifying the crucial variables.

An alternative framework for sensitivity analysis has appeared in the literature in attempting to measure the effect of errors in input estimates on value. While this analysis is examined in detail, it will be shown that this is actually a special case of the more general sensitivity analysis used in this study.

Finally, a paradigm is introduced and its variables selected and specified for use in this study. Chapter 5 presents this study's results and data analysis. A summary of the important findings concludes chapter 4.

General Characteristics of the Model

The model used in this study is a deterministic rate of return and valuation model. In light of the previous literature review, it is now assumed that since the model is deterministic, each result can be traced back to an original point estimate rather than to a range with associated probability distributions. Further, when its inputs are changed, the model is not assumed to account for risk but rather for uncertainty.

Although complex, the model can be solved analytically in all cases, with the exception of one. This special case occurs when solving for the internal rate of return but can be approximated by a trial-and-error sorting procedure. The computerization of this model will aid in providing identical solutions to those that are possible mathematically, although the computer will assist in terms of time, accuracy, and costliness.

The model is the well-known discounted cash flow model and thus can be used to make real estate investment decisions by providing information necessary to meet or fail criteria established by capital budgeting techniques. It can also be used to help understand the relationships among different variables in the investment decision. The model can be used "to analyze the sensitivity of the rates of return [and values] to changes in the values of input variables."[1] This, of course, is the main purpose of this study.

Assumptions of the Model

A number of assumptions about the model are necessary before its development. Many of these are discussed in Pyhrr.[2] A major assumption is that the equity valuation model is the best measure of rate of return and value for real estate investors. Most of the literature supports this claim and by adopting this basic assumption, the user is able to analyze ex ante real estate project data and make decisions based upon acceptable criteria.

It is also assumed that the assumptions necessary for the methodology of the model are valid. These include a yearly cash flow occurring at the end of each year rather than continuously and a reinvestment rate equal to the discount rate in the present value calculation or equal to the internal rate of return in the internal rate of return calculation; also included is the assumption that all the inputs are fixed or can be estimated with certainty. While each of these assumptions can be treated in alternative models, they are all implicit in the model used in this research.

A number of assumptions are also necessary regarding the use of this model in real-world investment decision-making. While it is quite clear that sophisticated financing arrangements, depreciation elections, or taxation treatment may be advantageous and allowable for some users, this model will not permit unusual or very complex programs other than those generally used. For example, in terms of real estate finance, the model will not permit wraparound financing, balloon payments, or multiple mortgages. This model is limited to level amortization of a single mortgage for various terms. Depreciation treatment will be limited to the well-known accelerated methods of depreciation and will not enable use of quick writeoffs, deferring recapture, or similarly recognized provisions. In addition, this model examines the income and capital tax effects of return in real estate and will not treat issues such as prepaid interest, tax-free exchanges, minimum tax considerations, income averaging, or other available techniques. Since the purpose of this model is to examine the sensitivity of various variables, it is felt that these assumptions are not too restrictive. A number of other models adequately treat many of these.[3]

The final assumption is, in some ways, the most crucial one. Since the estimates are certain, it is assumed that the inputs are correct as estimated based upon any available information at the time of the decision. This relates to all of the inputs: rents and expenses are assumed to be unchanged each year and are known precisely (although growth factors could easily handle this problem, but were purposely omitted since they would introduce further complications in the sensitivity analysis). The estimated selling price is assumed to be estimable based upon some estimate of an appreciation (or depreciation) rate at the time of sale, and the holding period is assumed to be known. While none of these is actually known, this (or any other) ex ante deterministic model rests on the belief that the best estimates at one decision point are always superior to random estimates at the same time. If not, then an ex ante model cannot be used. Since all economic forecasting implies the use of ex ante parameters, this objection is not regarded as too serious an objection for this model.

The Equity Valuation Model

The General Form

The valuation model used in this study is based primarily upon the work of Wendt and Cerf.[4] They concluded that "it is generally recognized that the after-tax return on equity is the most significant measure of real estate investment returns." Although originally formulated in 1965 by Wendt and Wong,[5] equation 4.1 is exactly the same equation as in Cooper,[6] Cooper and Morrison,[7] Cooper and Pyhrr,[8] and Pyhrr,[9] as well as Wendt and Cerf, and Wendt and Wong earlier, if (1) selling expenses are assumed to be zero or (2) selling prices are net of selling expenses. Soelberg and Stefaniak account for 5 percent selling expenses.[10]

$$E = \sum_{t=1}^{HP} \frac{ATCF_t}{(1+r)^t} + \frac{ATER_{HP}}{(1+r)^{HP}}$$

where E is the equity invested in the project, $ATCF_t$ is the after-tax cash flow per period t, $ATER_{HP}$ is the after-tax equity reversion at the end of the holding period HP, and r is the rate of return. (4.1)

After-tax cash flow can then be defined as follows:

$$ATCF_t = R_t - M_t - T_t$$

where R_t is the net operating income per period t, M_t is the amortization payment per period t, and T_t is the income tax allowance per period t. (4.2)

Since the amortization payment is the sum of the interest payment and the principal reduction payment,

$$M_t = I_t + A_t$$

where I_t is the interest payment on the amortized mortgage in period t, and A_t is the mortgage principal reduction payment per period t. (4.3)

$$ATCF_t = R_t - I_t - A_t - T_t \quad (4.4)$$

After-tax equity reversion can be defined as follows:

$$ATER_{HP} = P - SE - UPRIN - CGT$$

where P is the selling price at the end of the holding period, SE are the selling expenses associated with the sale, $UPRIN$ is the unpaid principal mortgage balance at the end of the holding period, and CGT is the capital gains tax associated with the sale. (4.5)

Capital gains taxation can be viewed as the sum of two components: the tax on the capital gain and the tax on the depreciation recaptured at the time of sale.

$$CGT = CGTX + RCTX$$

where $CGTX$ is the tax on the capital gain and $RCTX$ is the tax on the recaptured depreciation. (4.6)

$$ATER_{HP} = P - SE - UPRIN - (CGTX + RCTX) \quad (4.7)$$

Thus, equation 4.1 is frequently written as:

$$E = \sum_{t=1}^{HP} \frac{R_t - I_t - A_t - T_t}{(1 + r)^t} + \frac{P - SE - UPRIN - CGT}{(1 + r)^{HP}} \quad (4.8)$$

$$E = \sum_{t=1}^{HP} \frac{R_t - I_t - A_t - T_t}{(1 + r)^t} + \frac{P - SE - UPRIN - (CGTX + RCTX)}{(1 + r)^{HP}} \quad (4.9)$$

Derivation of ATCF

Each of the four components of equations 4.4 and 4.6 can be further specified and their components identified. (Operating expenses include fixed expenses, variable expenses, and replacement of reserves.)

$$R_t = EGI_t - OE_t$$

where EGI_t is effective gross income per period *t*, and OE_t is operating expenses per period *t*. (4.10)

$$EGI_t = GR_t - BD_t \tag{4.11}$$

$$GR_t = GPT_t - VAC_t$$

where GR_t is the gross rent per period *t*, BD_t is the bad debt allowance per period *t*, GPI_t is the gross possible income per period *t*, and VAC_t is the vacancy allowance per period *t*. (4.12)

By substitution,

$$EGI_t = GPI_t - VAC_t - BD_t \tag{4.13}$$

$$R_t = GPI_t - VAC_t - BD_t - OE_t \tag{4.14}$$

According to equation 4.3, the total amortization payment is the sum of the interest paid on the mortgage and the payment to reduce the principal amount of the loan. Mathematically, the annual payment can be calculated as follows:

$$M_t = \left[\frac{COUP}{1 - \dfrac{1}{(1 + COUP)^{TERM}}} \right] \cdot DEBT \tag{4.15}$$

$$DEBT = (COST) \cdot (L/V)$$

where *COUP* is the coupon rate of interest on the mortgage, *TERM* is the term of the loan, *DEBT* is the amount borrowed to finance the property, *COST* is the total cost of the property, and *L/V* is the loan to value ratio. (4.16)

To split the mortgage payment into its component parts, the interest payment is defined as follows:

$$I_t = (COUP)(DEBT) \qquad \text{where } t = 1 \tag{4.17}$$

$$I_t = (COUP)(PRIN_{t-1}) \qquad \text{where } t = 2, 3, \ldots, HP$$

where $PRIN_{t-1}$ is the remaining principal at the end of t–1 years, and HP is the holding period. (4.18)

And thus, by equation 4.3,

$$A_t = M_t - I_t \tag{4.19}$$

and substituting equations 4.15, 4.16, and 4.18 into equation 4.19,

$$A_t = \left\{ \left[\left(\frac{COUP}{1 - \dfrac{1}{(1 + COUP)^{TERM}}} \right) \cdot (COST) \cdot (L/V) \right] - [(COUP) \cdot (PRIN_{t-1})] \right\}$$

where $t > 1$. If $t = 1$, $(PRIN_{t-1}) = (DEBT)$. (4.20)

$$PRIN_t = (DEBT) - A_t \qquad \text{where } t = 1 \tag{4.21}$$

$$PRIN_t = PRIN_{t-1} - A_t \qquad \text{where } t = 2, 3, \ldots, HP$$

where $PRIN_t$ is the remaining principal at the end of t years. (4.22)

To compute the income tax allowance, we need to compute taxable income.

$$TINC_t = R_t - I_t - DEP_t$$

where $TINC$ is the taxable income per period t, and DEP_t is the depreciation allowance per period t. (4.23)

Since the depreciation method elected may vary according to (1) the type of property, (2) the age of the structure, according to the Tax Reform Act of 1969, and (3) managerial preference within the law, equations 4.24 through 4.27 enable the user to choose an allowable depreciation function.

$$DEP_t = f(DEP_{t\alpha}) \quad \text{if elected} \tag{4.24}$$

$$DEP_t = g(DEP_{t\beta}) \quad \text{if elected} \tag{4.25}$$

$$DEP_t = h(DEP_{t\gamma}) \quad \text{if elected} \tag{4.26}$$

$$DEP_t = i(DEP_{t\delta}) \quad \text{if elected}$$

where $DEP_{t\alpha}$ is the straight-line depreciation method per period t, $DEP_{t\beta}$ is the 125 percent declining balance depreciation method per period t, $DEP_{t\gamma}$ is the 150 percent declining balance depreciation method per period t, $DEP_{t\delta}$ is the 200 percent declining balance depreciation method per period t, and f, g, h, i are functional operators for the methods. (4.27)

Thus by substitution, equation 4.23 is equivalent to:

$$TINC_t = [(EGI_t - OE_t) - [(COUP)(PRIN_{t-1})] - DEP_t] \tag{4.28}$$

The income tax allowance is equal to taxable income times the (legal) investor's effective tax rate.

$$T_t = (TINC_t) \cdot (TRATE)$$

where $TRATE$ is the owner's effective tax rate. (4.29)

By substituting equation 4.28 into equation 4.29,

$$T_t = \{[(EGI_t - OE_t) - [(COUP)(PRIN_{t-1})] - DEP_t]\,(TRATE)\} \tag{4.30}$$

Finally, using equations 4.10, 4.18, 4.20, and 4.30, equation 4.4 can be written as follows:

$$ATCF_t = [(EGI_t - OE_t) - [(COUP)(PRIN_{t-1})]$$

$$- \left\{ \left[\left(\frac{COUP}{1 - \dfrac{1}{(1 + COUP)^{TERM}}} \right) \cdot (COST) \cdot (L/V) \right] \right.$$

$$- [(COUP)(PRIN_{t-1})] \Bigg\} - \{[(EGI_t - OE_t)$$

$$- [(COUP)(PRIN_{t-1})] - DEP_t] \, (TRATE)]\} \qquad (4.31)$$

Derivation of ATER

Equation 4.7, after-tax equity reversion, can be similarly specified and its components identified.

$$P = (COST) \cdot (1 + REVGR)$$

where $REVGR$ is the reversion growth rate for the entire holding period. (4.32)

$$SE = (P)x$$

where x is the percentage of selling price used to assess selling expenses. (4.33)

Using equation 4.21, the unpaid principal is the remaining principal balance at the end of the holding period and can be defined as:

$$UPRIN = DEBT - A_{HP}$$

where $UPRIN$ is the unpaid principal balance, and A_{HP} is the total mortgage principal reduction at the end of the holding period. (4.34)

Finally, since the computation of the capital gains tax is the sum of the tax on the capital gains and the tax on the recaptured depreciation by equation 4.6, each can be represented as follows:

$$CGTX = (CGTXR) \cdot (NGAIN)$$

where $CGTXR$ is the capital gains tax rate, and $NGAIN$ is the net gain. (4.35)

$$NGAIN = (GAIN) - (RECAP)$$

where $GAIN$ is the gain from the sale, and $RECAP$ is the amount of excess depreciation recaptured. (4.36)

The gain from the sale is calculated as follows:

$$GAIN = P - BASIS \tag{4.37}$$

$$BASIS = COST - ADEP \tag{4.38}$$

$$ADEP = \sum_{t=1}^{HP} DEP_t$$

where *BASIS* is the adjusted basis in the property, *ADEP* is the accumulated depreciation in the property. (4.39)

Then by substitution,

$$GAIN = P - COST - \sum_{t=1}^{HP} DEP_t \tag{4.40}$$

The depreciation subject to recapture is equal to the excess depreciation taken times the recapture percentage formula, as specified by the Internal Revenue Code.

$$RECAP = (EXDEP) \cdot (RECAP\%)$$

where *EXDEP* is excess depreciation, and *RECAP* percent is the recapture percentage formula. (4.41)

$$EXDEP = \sum_{t=1}^{HP} DEP_t - DEP_{HP\alpha} \tag{4.42}$$

$$RECAP\% = [1 - .12(HP - 8.33)]$$

where $DEP_{HP\alpha}$ is the accumulated straight-line depreciation at the end of the holding period. (4.43)

By substituting equations 4.42 and 4.43 into equation 4.41,

$$RECAP = \left(\sum_{t=1}^{HP}{}' \; DEP_t - DEP_{HP\alpha} \right) \cdot (1 - .12(HP - 8.33)) \tag{4.44}$$

and by substituting equations 4.40 and 4.44 into equation 4.36,

$$NGAIN = P - COST - \sum_{t=1}^{HP} DEP_t - \left(\sum_{t=1}^{HP} DEP_t - DEP_{HP\alpha} \right)$$

$$\cdot\ 1 - .12(HP - 8.33) \qquad (4.45)$$

Finally, equation 4.35 can now be rewritten as follows:

$$CGTX = CGTXR \cdot \left[P - COST - \sum_{t=1}^{HP} DEP_t - \left[\left(\sum_{t=1}^{HP} DEP_t - DEP_{HP\alpha} \right) \right.\right.$$

$$\left.\left. - (1 - .12(HP - 8.33)) \right] \right] \qquad (4.46)$$

The second component of the capital gains tax is the tax on the recaptured depreciation.

$$RCTX = (RCTXR) \cdot (RECAP)$$

where *RCTXR* is the recaptured depreciation tax rate. (4.47)

Using equation 4.44, this component can be rewritten as:

$$RCTX = RCTXR \left[\left(\sum_{t=1}^{HP} DEP_t - DEP_{HP\alpha} \right) (1 - .12(HP - 8.33)) \right] \qquad (4.48)$$

Thus by rewriting equation 4.6, using equations 4.46 and 4.48,

$$CGT = CGTXR \left[P - COST - \sum_{t=1}^{HP} DEP_t \right.$$

$$\left. - \left[\sum_{t=1}^{HP} DEP_t - DEP_{HP\alpha} \right) (1 - .12(HP - 8.33)) \right] \Bigg]$$

$$+ RCTXR \left[\left(\sum_{t=1}^{HP} DEP_t - DEP_{HP\alpha} \right) (1 - .12(HP - 8.33)) \right] \qquad (4.49)$$

Finally, using equations 4.32, 4.33, 4.34, and 4.49, equation 4.7 can be written as follows:

$$ATER_{HP} = [(COST) \cdot (1 + REVGR)] - [(P) \cdot x] - [DEBT - A_{HP}]$$
$$- \left\{ CGTXR \left[P - COST - \sum_{t=1}^{HP} DEP_t - \left[\left(\sum_{t=1}^{HP} DEP_t - DEP_{HP\alpha} \right) (1 - .12(HP - 8.33)) \right] \right] + RCTXR \left[\left(\sum_{t=1}^{HP} DEP_t - DEP_{HP\alpha} \right) (1 - .12(HP - 8.33)) \right] \right\} \quad (4.50)$$

The Completely Specified Model

After having specified all of the components of after-tax cash flow (equation 4.4) in equation 4.31, and all of the components of after-tax equity reversion (equation 4.7), in equation 4.50, the original equity valuation model, equation 4.1 can be respecified as follows:

$$E = \sum_{t=1}^{HP} \frac{1}{(1+r)^t} \left[(EGI_t - OE_t) - [(COUP)(PRIN_{t-1})] - \left\{ \left[\left(\frac{COUP}{1 - \frac{1}{(1 + COUP)^{TERM}}} \right) \cdot (COST) \cdot (L/V) \right] - [(COUP)(PRIN_{t-1})] \right\} - \{[(EGI_t - OE_t) - [(COUP)(PRIN_{t-1})] - DEP_t] \cdot (TRATE)\} \right]$$

$$+\frac{1}{(1+r)^{HP}}\Bigg\{[(COST)\cdot(1+REVGR)]-[(P)\cdot x]-[DEBT-A_{HP}]$$

$$-CGTXR\Bigg\{P-COST-\sum_{t=1}^{HP}\Bigg[DEP_t$$

$$-\Bigg[\Bigg(\sum_{t=1}^{HP}DEP_t-DEP_{HP\alpha}\Bigg)(1-.12(HP-8.33))\Bigg]\Bigg]\Bigg\}$$

$$+RCTXR\Bigg[\Bigg(\sum_{t=1}^{HP}DEP_t-DEP_{HP\alpha}\Bigg)(1-.12(HP-8.33))\Bigg]\Bigg\} \tag{4.51}$$

Table 4-1 summarizes the results of the model specifications presented above. Since this valuation model is time adjusted, the user calculates a present value amount for the equity value, E. This model can also be used to approximate the internal rate of return on equity, IRR, by setting E equal to the present value cost of acquiring the project, C, and solving for IRR.

$$O=\sum_{t=1}^{HP}\frac{ATCF_t}{(1+\mathrm{IRR})^t}+\frac{ATER_{HP}}{(1+\mathrm{IRR})^{HP}}-C \tag{4.52}$$

This study will use both forms of the discounted cash flow to equity model. In the next section, the mathematical results of changes in the function E will be examined as a result of changes in a number of important variables through the use of partial differentiation.

Theoretical Sensitivity Analysis

The Results

Since sensitivity analysis seeks to show the effect on output as a result of a change in an input variable, the general results may be derived through the use of the technique of partial differentiation. Thus, the partial derivative of the valuation model with respect to each of the variables in question would be equivalent to computerization of the model and the repeated calculation of the model under different input assumptions.

However, as has been pointed out in Carey and MacKinnon, certain derivatives may be quite complex for some variables. While they are conceivably solvable, it has been previously noted that "the manipulations necessary make a computer simulation an attractive alternative."[11]

In general,

$$\frac{\partial E}{\partial EGI_t} = \sum_{t=1}^{HP} \frac{1}{(1+r)^t} (1 - TRATE) \tag{4.53}$$

$$\frac{\partial E}{\partial OE_t} = \sum_{t=1}^{HP} - \frac{1}{(1+r)^t} (1 - TRATE) \tag{4.54}$$

$$\begin{aligned}\frac{\partial E}{\partial COST} &= \sum_{t=1}^{HP} \frac{1}{(1+r)^{HP}} \left[- \left(\frac{COUP}{1 - \frac{1}{(1+COUP)^{TERM}}} \right) \cdot (L/V) \cdot d(COST) \right] \\ &+ \frac{1}{(1+r)^{HP}} \{ dCOST[(1-x) \cdot (1+REVGR)] \\ &- CGTXR(1+REVGR)dCOST + (CGTXR)d(COST) \} \end{aligned} \tag{4.55}$$

$$\begin{aligned}\frac{\partial E}{\partial r} = \sum_{t=1}^{HP} \frac{-t}{(1+r)^{t+1}} dr \Bigg[& (EGI_t - OE_t) - [(COUP) \cdot (PRIN_{t-1})] \\ & - \left\{ \left[\left(\frac{COUP}{1 - \frac{1}{(1+COUP)^{TERM}}} \right) \cdot (COST)(L/V) \right] - [(COUP)(PRIN_{t-1})] \right\} \\ & - \{ [(EGI_t - OE_t) - [(COUP)(PRIN_{t-1})] - DEP_t] (TRATE) \} \Bigg]\end{aligned}$$

Table 4-1
Table of Model Specifications for Equity Valuation Model

	Equation
I. $E = \sum_{t=1}^{HP} \frac{ATCF_t}{(1+r)^t} + \frac{ATER_{HP}}{(1+r)^{HP}}$	(4.1)
II. $E = \sum_{t=1}^{HP} \frac{R_t - I_t - A_t - T_t}{(1+r)^t} + \frac{P - SE - UPRIN - CGT}{(1+r)^{HP}}$	(4.8)
III. $E = \sum_{t=1}^{HP} \frac{R_t - I_t - A_t - T_t}{(1+r)^t} + \frac{P - SE - UPRIN - (CGTX + RCTX)}{(1+r)^{HP}}$	(4.9)
IV. $E = \sum_{t=1}^{HP} \frac{1}{(1+r)^t} \left[(EGI_t - OE_t) - [(COUP)(PRIN_{t-1})] - \left\{ \left[\left(\frac{COUP}{1 - \frac{1}{(1+COUP)^{TERM}}} \right) (COST)(L/V) \right] - [(COUP)(PRIN_{t-1})] \right\} - \{[(EGI_t - OE_t) - [(COUP)(PRIN_{t-1})] - DEP_t]\ (TRATE)\} \right]$	

$$
\begin{aligned}
&+ \frac{1}{(1+r)^{HP}} \Bigg\{ [(COST)(1 + REVGR)] - [(P)x] - [DEBT - A_{HP}] \\
&- CGTXR \Bigg\{ P - COST - \sum_{t=1}^{HP} \left[DEP_t - \left[\left(\sum_{t=1}^{HP} DEP_t - DEP_{HP\alpha} \right) (1 - .12(HP - 8.33)) \right] \right] \Bigg\} \\
&+ RCTXR \left[\left(\sum_{t=1}^{HP} DEP_t - DEP_{HP\alpha} \right) (1 - .12(HP - 8.33)) \right] \Bigg\}
\end{aligned} \tag{4.51}
$$

$$- \frac{HP}{(1+r)^{HP+1}} dr \, \{[(COST) \cdot (1+REVGR)] - [(P) \cdot x] - [DEBT - A_{HP}]\}$$

$$- \left\{ CGTXR \left[P - COST - \sum_{t=1}^{HP} DEP_t \right. \right.$$

$$\left. - \left[\left(\sum_{t=1}^{HP} DEP_t - DEP_{HP\alpha} \right) (1 - .12(HP - 8.33)) \right] \right]$$

$$\left. + RCTXR \left[\left(\sum_{t=1}^{HP} DEP_t - DEP_{HP\alpha} \right) (1 - .12(HP - 8.33)) \right] \right\} \quad (4.56)$$

$$\frac{\partial E}{\partial REVGR} = \frac{1}{(1+r)^{HP}} [(COST)] \, d(REVGR) \quad (4.57)$$

$$\frac{\partial E}{\partial COUP} = (COST) \cdot (L/V)[COUP(1 - (1 + COUP)^{-TERM})^{-1}]$$
$$+ COUP[-(1 - (1 + COUP)^{-TERM})^{-2}$$
$$\cdot (TERM)(1 + COUP)^{TERM+1} \, d(COUP)] \quad (4.58)$$

$$\frac{\partial E}{\partial (L/V)} = \sum_{t=1}^{HP} \frac{1}{(1+r)^t} \left(\frac{COUP}{1 - \frac{1}{(1+COUP)^{TERM}}} \right) (COST) d(L/V) \quad (4.59)$$

$$\frac{\partial E}{\partial TERM} = \sum_{t=1}^{HP} \{(COUP) \cdot (COST) \cdot (L/V) - [(1 - (1 + COUP)^{-TERM})]^{-2}$$
$$\cdot [(-TERM)(1 + COUP)^{-TERM-1}]\} d(TERM) \quad (4.60)$$

$$\frac{\partial E}{\partial DEP_t} = \sum_{t=1}^{HP} \frac{1}{(1+r)^t} (TRATE) + \left[\frac{1}{(1+r)^{HP}} CGTXR(HP) \right.$$
$$\left. - HP(TCTXR)(1 - .12(HP - 8.33)) \right] dDEP_t \quad (4.61)$$

$$\frac{\partial E}{\partial TRATE} = \sum_{t=1}^{HP} \frac{1}{(1+r)^t} \{(EGI_t - OE_t)$$

$$- [(COUP)(PRIN_{t-1})] - DEP_t\} d(TRATE) \tag{4.62}$$

$$\frac{\partial E}{\partial HP} = \frac{1}{(1+r)^{HP}} \Bigg[(CGTXR)(ADEP - DEP_{HP})(.12)$$

$$+ (RCTXR)\left(\sum_{t=1}^{HP} DEP_t - DEP_{HP} \right)(.12) \Bigg] d(HP)$$

$$+ \Bigg[\Bigg\{ [(COST) \cdot (1 + REVGR)] - [(P) \cdot x] - [DEBT - A_{HP}]$$

$$- \Bigg\{ CGTXR \Bigg[P - COST - \sum_{t=1}^{HP} DEP_t$$

$$- \Bigg[\left(\sum_{t=1}^{HP} DEP_t - DEP_{HP\alpha} \right) (1 - .12(HP - 8.33)) \Bigg] \Bigg]$$

$$+ RCTXR \Bigg[\left(\sum_{t=1}^{HP} DEP_t - DEP_{HP\alpha} \right) (1 - .12(HP - 8.33)) \Bigg] \Bigg\} \Bigg\}$$

$$\cdot \{ -(1+r)^{-HP} \ln(1+r) \} \Bigg] d(HP) \tag{4.63}$$

$$\frac{\partial E}{\partial SE} = -\frac{1}{(1+r)^{HP}} (xdP + Pdx) \tag{4.64}$$

Table 4-2
Summary of Derivative Changes

Number	*Variable*	*Direction of Change in E*
1	*EGI*	$\partial E > 0$
2	*OE*	$\partial E < 0$
3	*COST*	$\partial E < 0$
4	*r*	$\partial E < 0$
5	*REVGR*	$\partial E > 0$
6	*COUP*	$\partial E < 0$
7	*L/V*	$\partial E > 0$[a]
8	*TERM*	$\partial E > 0$[a]
9	*DEP*	$\partial E > 0$[a]
10	*TRATE*	$\partial E < 0$
11	*HP*	$\partial E > 0$[a]
12	*SE*	$\partial E < 0$

[a]Assuming equity dividend rate, $y > k$, the cost of capital.

Summary of Derivative Changes

Table 4-2 presents a summary of the directions of changes as given in results above. For example, given a positive change in operating expenses, the resulting change will be negative. The partial derivatives also enable us to compute the magnitude of the changes as well. This is basically why sensitivity analysis is valuable. Since the direction of the change is usually clear, the magnitude is of more interest.

The results of the complete sensitivity analysis by computerization is presented in the next chapter. The results are analyzed on the basis of equal percentage changes in the variables under consideration. The summaries presented in table 4-2 merely indicate the direction rather than the magnitude of the changes, which can be found in the sensitivity tables in the next chapter.

Recent Contributions to Sensitivity Analysis Theory

A Brief History to 1973

Although sensitivity analysis has been performed frequently for many years in many areas, recent interest has focused on the development of a general framework or a theoretical approach to sensitivity analysis. Gau and Kohlhepp observed a similar development in their work on reinvestment rate sensitivity. They found that earlier work had focused on real estate investments on an ad hoc basis. This paper generalized sensitivity analysis for any investment data under consideration.[12] Gau and Kohlhepp's major contribution was to extend the analysis found in Joy and Bradley[13] to real estate investment analysis, with particular attention focused on the reinvestment rate used in the discounted cash flow model.

Prior to 1973, a few authors had tried to develop methodology for sensitivity studies and began to discuss the importance of this work. As early as 1958, Maffei viewed the necessity of distinguishing the "optimal-insensitive decision rule from the optimal-sensitive decision rule."[14] He suggested that additional research was necessary about the sensitivities of many well-known decision rules since he felt managers and analysts "had not delved far enough into the study of mathematical characteristics of the simplest decision rules."[15]

Sensitivity analysis as a technique was first discussed by Soloman,[16] Swalm,[17] House,[18] and Rappaport[19] in 1966-67. It was in these papers that the groundwork was set for more general and complete analysis. Soloman's paper presented graphs relating returns, holding periods, and rates of return for capital investment projects. He argued that theoretically correct choice criteria are limited in a practical sense due to the risk involved in making the estimates. Thus he focused on the effects of errors in estimation.[20] Swalm's comment suggested that the results of sensitivity studies were too narrow since they are data sensitive and generally relate to the project at hand.[21]

House examined the effect of errors in estimating input parameters between two possible capital investments: a pipeline project and an overseas investment venture. His perception of the sensitivity question was very concise. What sensitivity analysis must do, he discovered, was to establish where relatively small changes in estimates result in relatively large changes in rate of return. At that time, the analyst would know that the investment decision based upon the calculated rate of return would be sensitive to errors in those estimates.[22] In a similar sense, Rappaport viewed the importance of sensitivity analysis for the use of deciding whether or not to acquire additional information. If the variable under analysis is not critical, the analyst would not be interested in purchasing additional information to assist in the decision-making process.[23]

Two papers by Huefner continued to generalize the analysis of examining the effects of errors in cash flows.[24] In examining previous work, Huefner concluded that the results found by the researchers were generally "relevant only in the particular context for which they are computed."[25] It will be shown in this study that data sensitivity is an important consideration. Finally, Huefner suggested that more general analysis was needed and the emphasis should be on the decision model itself rather than on the specific situation.[26] Joy and Bradley's work represents a culmination of this strain up to 1973.

Others used sensitivity analysis in a variety of applications. Carey and MacKinnon[27] and Johnson and Carey[28] examined the sensitivity of equipment replacement valuation to investment credit policies. Gentry[29] advocated its use in analyzing cash budgeting policies for firms. Jansen,[30] Rappaport,[31] Glover,[32] and others used this method in mathematical programming problems.

In general, sensitivity analysis is well recognized, although traditionally not well understood. However, based upon the work of Joy and Bradley, Whisler presented a method which is the most general and useful to date. As an actual approach, it will be shown to be a special case of a complete sensitivity analysis, although very useful in helping decision makers account for uncertainty.

Whisler's Contribution

Whisler followed the tradition of analyzing the effect of errors in input parameters on internal rate of return.[33] He defined present value of an investment as

$$PV(i) = -D + \sum_{n=1}^{N} \frac{R_n}{(1+i)^n} \tag{4.65}$$

where D is the cost of the investment, R_n is the cash for periods 1, 2, . . . , N, and i is the discount rate. To measure changes in cash flow, Whisler defined d as the rate of constant decline in redefining R_n:

$$R_n = R(1-d)^{n-1} \tag{4.66}$$

for $n = 1, 2, \ldots, N$, with $0 \leqslant d < 1$. This is the same expression found in Joy and Bradley and the graphs presented in the 1973 paper represented sensitivities of the present value to changes in input parameters cash flow, project life, and rate of decline in cash flow.[34] Whisler presented an expression F_1 called the error factor, which extended the previous work.

Since percentage changes in rate of return due to percentage changes in the investment can be expressed as

$$\frac{dr}{r} \approx -\left(\frac{D(r+d)(1+r)}{r[D(r+d)N + D(1+r) - RN]}\right)\frac{dD}{D} \tag{4.67}$$

where $\approx$ means approximately equal to, Whisler defines F_1 equal to the function in parentheses.

$$\frac{dr}{r} = -F_1 \frac{dD}{D} \tag{4.68}$$

Thus, by computing the change in original investment, the analyst could examine the change in return as per the error factor.

Some real estate examples of Whisler's technique have been presented in another paper,[35] in which he examined the sensitivities of changes in rate of return to changes in cash flow. This can be represented in the following way:

percentage change in rate of return = (year n error factor)(percentage change in cash flow in year n)

$$\%\,\text{IRR} = \Delta(F_n) \cdot (\%\,\Delta CF_n) \tag{4.69}$$

The year n error factor, F_n, can be defined as

$$F_n = \frac{\text{cash flow in yr } n}{K \text{ factor}} \tag{4.70}$$

where

$$\text{cash flow in yr } n = \frac{R_n}{(1+r)^n}$$

$$K \text{ factor} = \sum_{i=1}^{n} A_n R_n$$

$$A_n = (nr)/(1+r)^{n+1}$$

Thus,

$$\frac{dr}{r} \approx \left(\frac{\dfrac{R_n}{(1+r)^n}}{\left[\displaystyle\sum_{i=1}^{n} \frac{nr}{(1+r)^{n+1}} \right] R_n} \right) \frac{dR_n}{R_n} \tag{4.71}$$

which is similar to the result from the previous paper. Whisler has also developed a set of tables for the A factor as an aid in using this technique. Thus, using his example case, if R_n = \$4,560, $n = 9$, and $r = .13$, then

$$\text{cash flow in yr } n = \frac{R_n}{(1+r)^n} = \$1{,}518$$

$$K \text{ factor} = \sum_{i=1}^{n} \frac{nr}{(1+r)^{n+1}} R_n = \$39{,}649$$

$$F_n = 0.0383$$

Thus, a 10 percent change in cash flow in the ninth year would cause only a .383 percent change in rate of return. Similar results could be obtained for different years, forecasts, and percentage changes.

Therefore, using this methodology, one can determine on a case by case basis whether errors in inputs will be significant or not as long as they affect cash flows. While the calculations are relatively simple and the cash flow data are known or estimated, this method is a very useful advancement in enabling users to identify those variables crucial in affecting returns.

The Usefulness of Whisler's Method

Whisler's approach is an approximation, but it is a suitable method to analyze real estate investment projects. Although it is more general than previous work in this area, it was not used for three reasons. First, it can only be used when the cash flows are changing. In the original exposition, the cash flows were supposed to be declining at a constant rate. Some of the variables investigated here do not affect cash flows and thus could not be examined in Whisler's framework. In this case, Whisler's method is a special case of a general sensitivity analysis.

The second limitation is that Whisler's method is a bit tedious, although computerization of the method could substantially alleviate the problem. In light of the first problem, the computer was used to pursue a complete sensitivity analysis which is more general than this approximation, even if it is computationally quite simple.

Finally, Whisler's method, although practical and enlightening, is actually no better than the complete methodology proposed below. It remains unclear whether the net benefits of this method exceed those derived by a general sensitivity analysis for the purposes outlined here, even if the first two problems are settled. The usefulness of this method as a practical tool remains a question for future research.

A Paradigm for a Complete Sensitivity Analysis

This study presents a complete sensitivity analysis in the sense that it examines the effects of changes in twelve major input variables on present value and internal rate of return. Obviously, a truly complete analysis would involve infinite positive and negative changes in every variable in the function. Even if one were to examine every variable in the function, it is impossible to analyze the magnitude of an infinite number of changes. Thus operationally, the analyst is forced to limit his complete analysis to a reasonable level. If the resulting analysis retained all of the important variables for a number of percentage changes, it would be known as a complete sensitivity analysis. Thus this thesis provides such an analysis for real estate investments.

Table 4-3 lists the twelve variables selected for testing in this study and groups those selected according to variable groups, as originally suggested by Walters (table 3-1). Each will be varied from its initial input value from -50 to +100 percent at 10 percent intervals. Thus each variable will be varied fifteen different times from its original value. The resulting changes form sensitivity functions for each variable. Behavioral data analysis is employed with the presentation of results in chapter 5.

For each measure, there are seven constants: bad debt allowance, vacancy allowance, growth in effective gross income, growth in operating expenses, selling expenses, capital gains tax rate, and the recapture tax rate. These variables were assumed to be held constant for one of two major reasons: they would either have no effect on the analysis (bad debt and vacancy allowances) or would interfere with the desired results (growth in effective gross income, growth in operating expenses, capital gains tax rate, and the recapture tax rate). Bad debt and vacancy allowances have the exact effect on effective gross income and thus are thought to be less interesting than some of the other variables. Further, since effective gross income is to be analyzed, those results will be sufficient to make judgments about the effect of bad debt and vacancy allowances.

Table 4-3
Input Variables by Variable Group
for Complete Sensitivity Analysis

Property management decisions
Effective gross income
Operating expenses
Purchase and sale decisions
Cost of property
Desired rate of return
Reversion growth rate
Fiscal, monetary, and housing policy decisions
Interest rate on mortgage
Loan to value ratio
Mortgage term
Taxation decisions
Depreciation method
Owner's effective tax rate
Depreciable life of property
Holding period

Two other variables to be held constant are growth in effective gross income and growth in operating expenses. While the effect of these variables on yield might be interesting, particularly in light of inflationary expectations, they will not aid in the testing of the thesis. The impact of these two factors can be significant in altering value or rate of return, but will be assumed to be zero. If they were allowed to enter the analysis, the results would be biased and would depend upon the size of the estimated growth rates. It has been shown elsewhere[36] that equal percentage increases in effective gross income and expenses will result in a higher value (or rate of return) than without the growth factors.

Selling expenses in this analysis were assumed to be zero or that the selling price was net of commissions, taxes, and fees. This is a typical assumption used by most investigators and is thought to be only a minor limitation. The effect of a change in selling expenses can be seen by a direct reduction in the selling price in dollars. Thus the effect of changes in expenses would have similar effects to equal percentage adjustments in selling expenses. Furthermore, it may not be unreasonable to assume that selling expenses in property are discounted by the investment market prior to sale. In that case, the analysis would be artificial.

The remaining factors to be held constant are the capital gains tax and the recapture tax rates. These factors have certainly been discussed at great length in much of the taxation literature. In addition, recent tax law reforms may have influenced some of the treatment of capital gains. However, unlike any of the variables to be tested, except the personal tax rate, these rates are established by the Internal Revenue Service and are not a function of the individual project. While the allowable depreciation method and depreciable life of the property are also subject to IRS regulation, the three tax rates are determined based upon the investor's other taxable income and the organizational form. It was felt that analysis of all of the rates would be superfluous and the effective regular rate would be sufficient.

Generally, previous writers have not provided an explanation for those parameters to be held constant. Cooper and Morrison, however, suggested that those to be held constant may be those that are determined by company policy.[37] They use depreciation method selection as a policy decision, whereas other writers and this study examine the effect of depreciation on the rate of return. It will also be assumed that either the cost of the property or the desired rate of return will be known for each internal rate of return or present value calculation, respectively. The various assumptions listed above will be maintained throughout the analysis.

Summary

This chapter specified the equity valuation model used in the analysis. While it is well known, few writers have examined the sensitivity of the model to changes in its parameters. This chapter specified the model in detail and reviewed various techniques available for sensitivity analysis.

The model has been completely specified so the user can observe precisely what is being measured. Using equation 4.51, the partial derivatives are provided for those variables under consideration. A summary of the directional changes has been provided.

A review and analysis has been made of other techniques of sensitivity analysis. Whisler's technique has been presented and an example provided. This technique has been shown to be an advancement whose usefulness has been questioned. Finally, a proposal was made for a complete sensitivity analysis. The results of this proposal are presented in chapter 5 and discussed in chapter 6.

Notes

1. Stephen A. Pyhrr, "A Proposed Model to Simulate Internal Rate of Return and Risk Characteristics of Investments in Multi-Family Rental Housing" (Ph.D. dissertation, University of Illinois at Urbana-Champaign, 1972) p. 52.

2. Ibid., pp. 53-56. See also Paul F. Wendt and Alan R. Cerf, *Real Estate Investment Analysis and Taxation* (New York: McGraw-Hill Book Co., 1969).

3. For example, see Owen K.S. Yoshimira and James R. Cooper, "Real Estate Investment Scanner Simulator (SCANNER)" (computer model, University of Illinois at Urbana-Champaign, 1974).

4. Wendt and Cerf, *Real Estate,* p. 26.

5. Paul F. Wendt and Sui N. Wong, "Investment Performance: Common Stocks Versus Apartment Houses," *Journal of Finance* 20 (December 1965): 633-646.

6. James R. Cooper, *Real Estate Investment Analysis* (Lexington, Mass.: Lexington Books, D.C. Heath and Co., 1974), pp. 107-163.

7. Cooper and Morrison, in Cooper, Real Estate, p. 88.

8. Cooper and Pyhrr, in Cooper, Real Estate, p. 65.

9. Pyhrr, "A Proposed Model," pp. 47-86.

10. Peer Soelberg and Norbert J. Stefaniak, "Impact of the Proposed Tax Reform Bill on Real Estate Investments," *The Appraisal Journal* 38 (April 1966): 188-211.

11. Kenneth Carey and Ian MacKinnon, "Sensitivity Analysis of an Equipment Replacement Model," *Proceedings of the Fifth Annual Meeting of the American Institute for Decision Sciences* (November 14-16, 1973): 19.

12. George W. Gau and Daniel B. Kohlhepp, "Reinvestment Rates and Sensitivity of Rates of Return in Real Estate Investment," *American Real Estate and Urban Economics Journal* 4 (Winter 1976): 69.

13. O. Maurice Joy and Jerry O. Bradley, "A Note on Sensitivity Analysis of Rates of Return," *Journal of Finance* 28 (December 1973): 1255-1261.

14. Richard B. Maffei, "Simulation, Sensitivity and Management Decision Rules," *The Journal of Business* 31 (July 1958): 186.

15. Ibid., p. 178.

16. Martin B. Soloman, Jr., "Uncertainty and Its Effect on Capital Investment Analysis," *Management Science* 12 (April 1966): 334-339.

17. Ralph O. Swalm, "A Review of 'Uncertainty and Its Effect on Capital Investment Analysis'," *The Engineering Economist* 12 (Winter 1967): 123-125.

18. William C. House, Jr., "The Usefulness of Sensitivity Analysis in Capital Investment Decision Making," *Management Accounting* 47 (February 1966): 22-29.

19. Alfred Rappaport, "Sensitivity Analysis in Decision Making," *The Accounting Review* 42 (July 1967), 441-456.

20. Soloman, "Capital Investment Analysis," p. 279.

21. Swalm, "Review of Uncertainty," p. 125.

22. House, "Usefulness of Sensitivity Analysis," p. 22.

23. Rappaport, "Sensitivity Analysis," p. 186.

24. Ronald J. Heufner, "Analyzing and Reporting Sensitivity Data," *The Accounting Review* 46 (October 1971): 717-732; idem, "Sensitivity Analysis and Risk Evaluation," *Decision Sciences* 3 (July 1972): 126-135.

25. Huefner, "Sensitivity Data," p. 717.

26. Ibid.

27. Carey and MacKinnon, "Sensitivity Analysis," pp. 18-21.

28. Glenn L. Johnson and Kenneth J. Carey, "The Effect of the Investment Credit on Equipment Replacement Decisions," *National Tax Journal* 23 (September 1970): 307-314.

29. James A. Gentry, "Linking the Cash Budgeting Process to the Capital Investment Process Through Simulation," *1973 AIDS Proceedings* 5 (November 1973): 14-17.

30. Robert E. Jansen, "Sensitivity Analysis and Integer Linear Programming," *The Accounting Review* 43 (July 1968): 425-426.

31. Alfred Rappaport, "Integer Programming and Managerial Analysis," *The Accounting Review* 44 (April 1969): 297-299.

32. Fred Glover, "Managerial Decision and Integer Programming," *The Accounting Review* 44 (April 1969): 300-303.

33. William D. Whisler, 1976, pp. 63-69.

34. Joy and Bradley, "Note on Sensitivity Analysis," pp. 1257-1259.

35. William D. Whisler, 1977, pp. 35-48.

36. Austin J. Jaffe, "A Reexamination of the Problem of Management Fee Assessment" (Working Paper, University of Illinois at Urbana-Champaign, 1976).

37. Cooper and Morrison, in Cooper, Real Estate, p. 89.

5 Data Analysis and Presentation of Results

Introduction

This chapter presents the results of the sensitivity study proposed in chapter 4. After a discussion of the data sources for selection of parameter and variable values, each of the tested variables' results is presented. Using the typical-project approach but basing the typical project on historical data, each variable's impact has been measured for changes in value and in rate of return. The dollar amount of change in value and the absolute percentage change in return have been converted to percentage changes. These percentage changes have been tabled as sensitivity functions for each variable.

A brief discussion of the relevance of behavioral data to sensitivity analyses follows the results. A summary of the results concludes the chapter.

Sources of Data

To achieve meaningful results in this analysis, particular attention was directed to the selection of data and the quality of data sources. This analysis led to the investigation of data sensitivity, which is summarized in chapter 6. Since good data are relatively difficult to find, many of the parameters were used on an ad hoc basis. Furthermore, with few exceptions and clarifications, the analysis of the sensitivity of data demonstrates that the magnitude of the results will tend to vary dependent upon the initial data, but the relative sensitivity of the variables tends to remain constant.

Property Management Variables

The two variables examined were effective gross income (*EGI*) and operating expenses (*OE*). The Institute of Real Estate Management publishes the results of annual surveys for income and expense data.[1] These figures when tabulated and edited provide an acceptable time series for various types of real property. Table 5-1 summarizes the income and expense data used in this analysis.

A quick analysis of the income and expense data reveals that on average,

Table 5-1
Average Income and Expense Data, Walkup Apartment Buildings

	EGI (Dollars/Room/ Annum)	*Percent of GPI (Percent/Room)*	*OE (Dollars/Room/ Annum)*	*Percent of EGI (Percent/Room)*
1957[a]	287.54	97.40	149.69	52.06
1958[b]	334.07	98.30	167.28	50.07
1959[c]	270.22	97.59	137.02	50.70
1960[c]	197.22	97.43	103.58	52.52
1961[c]	293.20	96.10	151.93	51.82
1962[c]	288.55	93.99	143.33	49.67
1963	N/A	N/A	N/A	N/A
1964	N/A	N/A	N/A	N/A
1965[d]	267.38	95.85	143.83	53.79
1966[d]	282.22	94.77	158.50	56.16
1967[d]	309.87	95.88	170.18	54.92
1968	N/A	N/A	N/A	N/A
1969[d]	353.44	96.45	201.55	57.03
1970[d]	367.16	97.08	208.57	56.81
1971[d]	391.59	96.78	218.47	55.79
1972[d]	391.75	96.43	213.64	54.53
1973[d]	409.57	96.09	213.65	52.16
1974[d]	453.37	95.22	237.30	52.34
1975[d]	461.94	95.34	243.91	52.80
Typical	335.00	96.30	180.00	53.40

Calculated from: Institute of Real Estate Management: *Apartment Building Experience Exchange of Rental Income and Operating Expense Data,* 1957–62, 1965; *Apartment Building Income-Expense Analysis,* 1966–67, 1969–72; and *Income-Expense Analysis,* 1973–75. All data reported for the previous years. N/A denotes not available.
[a]All types of apartment buildings (including Canada).
[b]All walkup apartment buildings (including Canada).
[c]All walkup buildings under 25 units (including Canada).
[d]All walkup apartment buildings with 12–24 units (excluding Canada).

income and expenses have varied over time. Furthermore, and perhaps more importantly, when stated as percentages of gross and effective incomes, the variations have been more pronounced and more difficult to explain. This is examined further in a later section.

Based upon the data, the initial case was selected with $335 rentable space per room, or $1,675 rentable space per apartment. If we examine a hypothetical project with twenty units, the monthly rent per unit would be $140. The total monthly rent would then be $2,800.

The average operating expense ratio was 53.4 percent of effective gross income. A recent paper examined the relationship between the operating expense ratio and valuation and found the operating expense to be of crucial significance.[2] Thus in this study, the operating expense ratio used was 53.4 percent, although the range varied from 49 to 57 percent.

Purchase and Sale Variables

These variables include the building cost (*COST*), the required rate of return (r), and the reversion growth rate (*REVGR*). Time series data for these variables are largely nonexistent, with the possible exception of construction cost estimates. However, the estimates chosen appear to conform to reality and have been typically adopted elsewhere.

Using time-adjusted building cost manuals, the cost of investment property of this type was initially input as $20 per square foot. The cost of the land was valued separately. The value of the land was derived using the same ratio of land to building as found in Gallagher's and Walters' studies. Thus, given the total cost of the property and the land/building ratio, and using the estimated cost of construction per square foot, an amount for the size of the building (8,085 square feet) and the value of the land ($83,300) were derived.

A variable that is difficult to measure accurately is r. Perhaps the best source for real estate projects is Roulac,[3] who provides an excellent review of studies of rates of return in real property. His results are inconclusive in that many of the studies cited are not strictly comparable, but he suggests 10 percent might be a representative figure. He stresses a lack of good data prohibits a careful investigation.

A formal set of data has yet to be found for *REVGR*. However, in view of the earlier discussion regarding additional problems encountered in light of various growth rates, the introduction of ex ante growth rate estimates based upon ex post data would probably have been discarded in this study. If not, interpretation would have been subject to the observed change in the reversion. Thus, the initial growth rate in the equity reversion was assumed to be zero, although in reality it is suspected to be positive.

Fiscal, Monetary, and Housing Policy Variables

Three variables are classified under this category: the interest rate on the conventional mortgage (*COUP*), the loan to value ratio (*L*/*V*), and the maturity or term of the mortgage (*TERM*). Table 5-2 shows the ranges for these variables. The typical value is the average of the series and serves as the value in the initial case in this study.

It is well known that the mortgage interest rate varies according to money

Table 5-2
Average Single-family Mortgage Rates, Loan to Value Ratios, and Terms[a]

	COUP *(Percent)*	*L/V* *(Percent)*	*TERM* *(Years)*
1963	5.84	73.3	24.0
1964	5.78	74.1	24.8
1965	5.76	74.1	24.8
1966	6.14	73.0	24.7
1967	6.33	73.6	25.2
1968	6.83	73.9	25.5
1969	7.66	72.8	25.5
1970	8.27	71.7	25.1
1971	7.60	74.3	26.2
1972	7.45	76.8	27.2
1973	7.78	77.3	26.3
1974	8.71	74.3	26.3
1975	8.75	74.7	26.8
1976	8.76	74.2	27.2
Typical	7.25	74.2	25.0

Source: *Federal Reserve Bulletin.* Washington, D.C.: Board of Governors of the Federal Reserve System, vol. 52–63 (July 1966–March 1976).

[a]All averages based upon statistical sampling.

and capital market pressure and that volatility is common. The time series reported in table 5-2 shows a steady increase during the late 1960s and early 1970s. The movement toward less regulated financial institutions and markets expected in the future will enable rates to vary even greater, provided market conditions warrant such changes. In any event, for the initial case, 7.25 percent was used for the percentage rate of interest.

The loan to value ratio appeared to center around 74 percent historically. In addition, it is felt that this ratio typically varies as high as .80 for income property, and frequently higher for single-family residences. The *Income Property Finance Report* has recently verified these contentions by reporting the policies of Connecticut Mutual Life Insurance (CM)[4] and Mutual Life Insurance Company of New York (MONY)[5] of maintaining .80 and .75 L/V ratios, respectively. Similar findings were found in a different context by Winger.[6]

The term of the mortgage was twenty-five years historically. This has been verified by the *Income Property Finance Report,* although currently some mortgages are amortized for twenty-eight to thirty years. The trend in the data suggests this result as well.

Taxation Variables

The final four variables have been classified as taxation (or accounting) variables: the elected depreciation method (*DEP*), the effective tax rate on income (*TRATE*), the depreciable life of the improvements (*LIFE*), and the expected holding period (*HP*). Historical data are very limited for these variables, although for our purposes, little problem exists.

The allowable depreciation methods are well known and much interest has been generated over the proper use of this technique in real estate investment analysis. In this analysis, all the major methods were examined, with the exception of "sum of the years digits." In the initial case, straight-line depreciation was adopted.

The question of whether to use marginal or effective tax rates as inputs for real estate investment projects remains unanswered. Cooper,[7] Messner, Schreiber, and Lyon,[8] and Roulac[9] apparently suggest the effective rate, although it is unknown or only poorly estimable. Therefore, by using the *1977 US Master Tax Guide* and examining the table of marginal tax rates for married couples filing jointly, a typical effective tax rate would be 39.35 percent. The rate would be less if the skewed distribution of income earners is considered. However, in this study a rate of 35 percent was used for two reasons: at 35 percent, the study would treat those investors in the highest tax bracket, and it was felt that ownership of investment property was not a typically attractive investment option for lower-income investors.

Guidelines are published by the Internal Revenue Service for depreciable lives for apartments. While ranges are suggested for some assets, paragraph 1168N of the *1977 US Master Tax Guide* reports forty years as the acceptable depreciable life for multiple-family real property.

Finally, historical data are apparently nonexistent for the average holding period in investment property. It has been commonly assumed to be eight to ten years by many authors since the effects of accelerated depreciation and maintenance-free management have appeared to conclude about that time in the life of the project.[10] Friedman concluded that ten years is a typical input as well, in a dissertation that attempted to determine the optimum holding period.[11]

Therefore, for each of the variables examined in this study, an attempt has been made to select correct initial values in determining the typical project. However, it could be argued that measures which take into account the upward trend in the data could be used and might better represent a typical project. This might also account for the fact that the data indicated an unfavorable project, as discussed below. By using values which reflect the upward trends in the variables, the analysis could be completed with more favorable and possibly more realistic amounts.

Although the typical-project approach was used in Gallagher's and Walters' studies, the data selected were purely ad hoc. Using carefully examined data, the results may be more unbiased and less prone to problems due to sensitivity of data sources.

A comparison between the data used by Walters and the data used in this study suggests that the typical project reported by Walters may not be very typical. Although most of his inputs seem reasonable, they do not appear to be supported by the historical data. Further, the sensitivities of the variables may be related to original input size. This problem is beyond the scope of this study, but remains a question for future research.

Summary of Typical-project Values

Based upon the discussion above and upon constant parameter assumptions discussed in chapter 4, table 5-3 lists the inputs used in this study. Then by

Table 5-3
Summary of Typical-project Inputs for Sensitivity Analyses

Variables	*Number*	*Values*
EGI	1	$2,800 per month
OE	2	53.4%
COST	3	$20 per square foot
r	4	10%
REVGR	5	0% per year
COUP	6	7.25%
L/V	7	74.2%
TERM	8	25 years
DEP	9	straight line method
TRATE	10	35%
LIFE	11	40 years
HP	12	10 years
Constants		*Values*
Bad debt allowance		0% per year
Vacancy allowance		0% per year
Growth in *EGI*		0% per year
Growth in *OE*		0% per year
Selling expenses		selling price as net
Capital gains tax rate		35%
Cost of land		$83,300
Size of building		8,085 square feet
Depreciable basis		75%

calculating the discounted present value (PV) and the internal rate of return (IRR) using these inputs, the results are as follows:

	PV	IRR
Typical project	$31,824.10	2.87%

Therefore, using available data sources and choosing best guess estimates where no data exist, the typical real estate project, by itself, is a relatively unattractive project. Since the rate of interest on the mortgage was considerably higher than 2.87 percent, negative financial leverage appears in the returns in this project. The results in the appendix confirm the belief that data sensitivity is a problem in the analysis if data-free sensitivities are desired. To the extent that the relative ranking in importance of each of the variables remains fairly constant, the analysis is free of data problem considerations. In that sense, therefore, the typical project, as valued using historical data, remains an unfavorable one, although comparisons can be made between it and more valuable projects. In fact, if the data analysis is correct, this may be further evidence of the low internal rates of return that most researchers have found using similar assumptions.

Presentation of Sensitivity Analyses

Tables 5-4 through 5-15 present the results of the complete sensitivity analysis described in chapter 4. Each variable has been varied a maximum of fifteen times at 10 percent intervals. With the exception of two variables (*COST* and *r*), each variable has been examined and sensitivity functions drawn for both present values and internal rates of return. The variable *DEP* has been tested at those points allowable by law.

In some cases, the typical percentage changes exceeded either the limits of the computerized model or rational real-world behavior. If the results were possible conceptually but not available, N/A can be found in place of the result. A dash indicates no meaningful result could be found. Tables 5-16 and 5-17 summarize the percentage changes for present values and internal rates of return. The analysis of the results is the primary subject of chapter 6.

The Relevance of Behavioral Data Analysis

One question that arises in any sensitivity analysis is similar to the management scientist's remark that sensitivity analysis was like the question "what if . . .?" In essence, the technique of sensitivity analysis asks many "what if" questions

Table 5-4
***EGI* Sensitivity Functions, Series 1**

Percent	*PV (Dollars)*	*Percent Δ*	*IRR (Percent)*	*Percent Δ*
-50	(16,055.94)[a]	(150.45)	(7.47)	(360.28)
-40	(6,435.02)	(120.22)	(5.43)	(289.20)
-30	3,185.90	(89.99)	(3.37)	(217.42)
-20	12,806.82	(59.76)	(1.29)	(144.95)
-10	22,427.73	(29.53)	0.81	(71.78)
0	31,824.73	0.00	2.87	0.00
10	39,737.16	24.86	4.61	60.63
20	45,990.76	44.52	6.03	110.10
30	52,244.36	64.17	7.46	159.93
40	58,497.95	83.82	8.91	210.45
50	64,751.55	103.47	10.36	260.97
60	71,005.14	123.12	11.82	311.85
70	77,258.74	142.77	13.29	363.07
80	83,512.34	162.42	14.77	414.63
90	89,765.93	182.07	16.26	466.55
100	98,019.54	201.72	17.75	518.47

[a]Parentheses indicate negative values.

Table 5-5
***OE* Sensitivity Functions, Series 2**

Percent	*PV (Dollars)*	*Percent Δ*	*IRR (Percent)*	*Percent Δ*
-50	69,314.26	117.80	11.42	297.91
-40	62,201.80	95.46	9.77	240.42
-30	54,955.15	72.68	8.09	181.88
-20	47,842.69	50.33	6.45	124.74
-10	40,596.03	27.56	4.80	67.25
0	31,824.10	0.00	2.87	0.00
10	21,106.40	(33.68)	0.52	(81.88)
20	9,957.70	(68.70)	(1.91)	(166.55)
30	(984.54)[a]	(103.09)	(4.27)	(248.78)
40	(12,133.25)	(138.13)	(6.64)	(331.36)
50	(23,075.49)	(172.51)	N/A	N/A
60	(34,017.74)	(206.89)	N/A	N/A
70	N/A	N/A	N/A	N/A
80	N/A	N/A	N/A	N/A
90	N/A	N/A	N/A	N/A
100	N/A	N/A	N/A	N/A

[a]Parentheses indicate negative values.

Table 5-6
***COST* Sensitivity Functions, Series 3**

Percent	*PV (Dollars)*	*Percent Δ*	*IRR (Percent)*	*Percent Δ*
-50	N/A	N/A	10.03	249.48
-40	N/A	N/A	8.19	185.37
-30	N/A	N/A	6.63	131.01
-20	N/A	N/A	5.31	85.02
-10	N/A	N/A	4.16	44.95
0	N/A	N/A	2.87	0.00
10	N/A	N/A	1.56	(45.64)
20	N/A	N/A	0.35	(87.80)
30	N/A	N/A	(0.73)[a]	(125.44)
40	N/A	N/A	(1.70)	(159.23)
50	N/A	N/A	(2.57)	(189.55)
60	N/A	N/A	(3.35)	(216.72)
70	N/A	N/A	(4.07)	(241.81)
80	N/A	N/A	(4.72)	(264.50)
90	N/A	N/A	(5.32)	(285.37)
100	N/A	N/A	(5.87)	(304.53)

[a]Parentheses indicate negative values.

Table 5-7
***r* Sensitivity Functions, Series 4**

Percent	*PV (Dollars)*	*Percent Δ*	*IRR (Percent)*	*Percent Δ*
-50	51,292.53	61.18	N/A	N/A
-40	46,552.95	46.28	N/A	N/A
-30	42,283.76	32.87	N/A	N/A
-20	38,434.75	20.77	N/A	N/A
-10	34,961.41	9.86	N/A	N/A
0	31,824.10	0.00	N/A	N/A
10	28.987.92	(8.91)[a]	N/A	N/A
20	26,421.75	(16.98)	N/A	N/A
30	24,097.87	(24.28)	N/A	N/A
40	21,991.72	(30.90)	N/A	N/A
50	20,080.88	(36.90)	N/A	N/A
60	18,347.01	(42.35)	N/A	N/A
70	16,771.36	(47.30)	N/A	N/A
80	15,338.84	(51.80)	N/A	N/A
90	14,035.47	(55.90)	N/A	N/A
100	12,848.75	(59.63)	N/A	N/A

[a]Parentheses indicate negative values.

Table 5-8
***REVGR* Sensitivity Functions, Series 5**

Percent	*PV (Dollars)*	*Percent Δ*	*IRR (Percent)*	*Percent Δ*
-50	N/A	N/A	N/A	N/A
-40	N/A	N/A	N/A	N/A
-30	8,941.64	(71.90)[a]	(8.53)	(397.21)
-20	18,387.45	(42.22)	(2.36)	(182.23)
-10	25,684.33	(19.29)	0.78	(72.82)
0	31,824.10	0.00	2.87	0.00
10	37,963.87	19.29	4.65	62.02
20	44,103.65	38.59	6.18	115.33
30	50,243.42	57.88	7.55	163.07
40	56,383.19	77.17	8.77	205.57
50	62,522.96	96.46	9.88	244.25
60	68,662.73	115.76	10.90	279.79
70	74,802.51	135.05	11.84	312.54
80	80,942.28	154.34	12.72	343.21
90	87,082.05	173.64	13.54	371.78
100	93,221.82	192.93	14.30	398.26

[a]Parentheses indicate negative values

Table 5-9
***COUP* Sensitivity Functions, Series 6**

Percent	*PV (Dollars)*	*Percent Δ*	*IRR (Percent)*	*Percent Δ*
-50	55,016.73	72.88	8.23	186.76
-40	50,951.25	60.10	7.32	155.05
-30	46,711.33	46.78	6.35	121.25
-20	42,420.78	33.30	5.34	86.06
-10	37,871.00	19.00	4.27	48.78
0	31,824.10	0.00	2.87	0.00
10	24,577.87	(22.78)	1.17	(59.23)
20	17,112.87	(46.23)	(0.63)	(121.95)
30	9,456.21	(70.29)	(2.51)	(187.46)
40	1,826.96	(94.26)	(4.42)	(254.01)
50	(5,978.10)[a]	(118.78)	(6.41)	(323.34)
60	(13,737.13)	(143.17)	N/A	N/A
70	(21,658.20)	(168.06)	N/A	N/A
80	(29,517.49)	(192.75)	N/A	N/A
90	N/A	N/A	N/A	N/A
100	N/A	N/A	N/A	N/A

[a]Parentheses indicate negative values.

Table 5-10
***L/V* Sensitivity Functions, Series 7**

Percent	*PV* (*Dollars*)	*Percent* Δ	*IRR* (*Percent*)	*Percent* Δ
-50	96,858.22	204.35	4.01	39.72
-40	84,217.44	164.63	3.93	36.93
-30	71,576.68	124.91	3.82	33.10
-20	58,765.09	84.66	3.68	28.22
-10	46,024.66	44.62	3.47	20.91
0	31,824.10	0.00	2.87	0.00
10	16,773.59	(47.29)	1.65	(41.81)
20	1,498.52	(95.29)	(0.58)	(120.21)
30	(13,982.96)[a]	(148.94)	(5.50)	(291.64)
40	N/A	N/A	N/A	N/A

[a]Parentheses indicate negative values.

Table 5-11
***TERM* Sensitivity Functions, Series 8**

Percent	*PV* (*Dollars*)	*Percent* Δ	*IRR* (*Percent*)	*Percent* Δ
-50	23,044.73	(27.59)[a]	3.58	24.74
-40	26,279.55	(17.42)	3.42	19.16
-30	28,453.93	(10.59)	3.27	13.94
-20	29,975.65	(5.81)	3.13	9.06
-10	31,055.45	(2.42)	3.00	4.53
0	31,824.10	0.00	2.87	0.00
10	32,367.75	1.71	2.75	(4.18)
20	32,745.84	2.90	2.63	(8.36)
30	33,000.87	3.70	2.51	(12.54)
40	33,201.07	4.33	2.41	(16.03)
50	33,363.65	4.84	2.33	(18.82)
60	33,496.37	5.25	2.25	(21.60)
70	33,605.35	5.60	2.19	(23.69)
80	33,695.10	5.88	2.14	(25.44)
90	33,769.23	6.11	2.10	(26.83)
100	33,830.68	6.31	2.06	(28.22)

[a]Parentheses indicate negative values.

Table 5-12
***DEP* Sensitivity Functions, Series 9**

Percent	*PV* (*Dollars*)	*Percent* Δ	*IRR* (*Percent*)	*Percent* Δ
0	31,824.10	0.00	2.87	0.00
25	31,677.26	(0.46)[a]	2.83	(1.39)
50	31,657.11	(0.52)	2.82	(1.74)
100	28,748.12	(9.67)	1.87	(34.84)

[a]Parentheses indicate negative values.

Table 5-13
***TRATE* Sensitivity Functions, Series 10**

Percent	*PV (Dollars)*	*Percent Δ*	*IRR (Percent)*	*Percent Δ*
-50	31,936.37	0.35	2.907	1.15
-40	31,913.92	0.28	2.900	0.90
-30	31,891.47	0.21	2.894	0.70
-20	31,869.01	0.14	2.887	0.45
-10	31,846.56	0.07	2.880	0.21
0	31,824.10	0.00	2.874	0.00
10	31,801.65	(0.07)[a]	2.867	(0.24)
20	31,779.19	(0.14)	2.860	(0.49)
30	31,756.73	(0.21)	2.853	(0.73)
40	31,734.28	(0.28)	2.847	(0.94)
50	31,711.82	(0.35)	2.840	(1.18)
60	31,689.37	(0.42)	2.833	(1.43)
70	31,666.91	(0.49)	2.826	(1.67)
80	31,644.45	(0.56)	2.820	(1.88)
90	31,622.00	(0.64)	2.813	(2.12)
100	31,599.54	(0.71)	2.806	(2.37)

[a]Parentheses indicate negative values.

Table 5-14
***LIFE* Sensitivity Functions, Series 11**

Percent	*PV (Dollars)*	*Percent Δ*	*IRR (Percent)*	*Percent Δ*
-50	26,593.70	(16.44)[a]	1.109	(61.41)
-40	28,412.02	(10.72)	1.753	(39.00)
-30	29,710.81	(6.64)	2.191	(23.76)
-20	30,684.91	(3.58)	2.510	(12.67)
-10	31,376.02	(1.41)	2.730	(5.01)
0	31,824.10	0.00	2.874	0.00
10	32,110.99	0.90	2.969	3.31
20	32,277.88	1.43	3.030	5.43
30	32,353.93	1.66	3.067	6.72
40	32,367.48	1.71	3.088	7.45
50	32,320.92	1.56	3.096	7.72
60	32,253.50	1.35	3.096	7.72
70	32,149.93	1.02	3.089	7.48
80	32,044.08	0.69	3.081	7.20
90	31,949.38	0.39	3.074	6.96
100	31,864.15	0.13	3.067	6.72

[a]Parentheses indicate negative values.

Table 5-15
***HP* Sensitivity Functions, Series 12**

Percent	*PV (Dollars)*	*Percent Δ*	*IRR (Percent)*	*Percent Δ*
-50	43,688.12	37.28	2.24	(21.95)
-40	40,870.70	28.43	2.38	(17.07)
-30	38,326.45	20.43	2.52	(12.20)
-20	35,994.62	13.10	2.65	(7.67)
-10	33,833.38	6.28	2.76	(3.83)
0	31,824.10	0.00	2.87	0.00
10	29,950.69	(5.89)[a]	2.97	3.48
20	28,198.59	(11.39)	3.06	6.62
30	26,554.99	(16.56)	3.14	9.14
40	25,008.71	(21.42)	3.22	12.20
50	23,549.69	(26.00)	3.30	14.98
60	22,169.08	(30.34)	3.37	17.42
70	20,859.16	(34.45)	3.44	19.86
80	19,612.90	(38.37)	3.50	21.95
90	18,424.28	(42.11)	3.56	24.04
100	17,288.01	(45.68)	3.62	26.13

[a]Parentheses indicate negative values.

and traditionally concludes the study based upon the answers derived. However, the argument made here is that the results of the study are relevant only in light of expected or possible deviations from the initial case. Therefore, an analysis of historical data to be used as a basis for expected future deviations is very relevant in determining whether the sensitivity analysis (and function) is meaningful within the framework of real-world observations. This section is directed to this point to determine the relevance of theoretical sensitivities.

The property management variables, *EGI* and *OE*, historically have varied significantly, even when looking at the mean data in table 5-1. Since it is reasonable to assume that individual projects could vary substantially more than the mean values, it would be reasonable to suggest that *EGI* and *OE* have tended to vary over time in light of ranges from -42 to +38 percent for *EGI* averages and -6.25 to +6.80 percent for *OE* averages. It has just been shown that changes in either of these variables have a dramatic impact on yield. In light of those results, it can therefore be concluded that these variables are significantly important as verified by the ranges found in the past data.

The purchase and sale variables, *COST*, *r*, and *REVGR*, are more difficult to assess. As previously noted, a good data base does not exist for these variables. However, many writers have suggested that *COST* has continued to increase as a result of inflationary prices or rising labor costs, or both. Therefore, cost estimates most likely have not been constant and will no doubt continue to rise in the future. For the individual project, the theoretical sensitivity function is

Table 5-16

Summary of Present Value Percentage Changes for Twelve Variables

Percent	*EGI*	*OE*	*COST*	*r*	*REVGR*	*COUP*	*L/V*	*TERM*	*DEP*	*TRATE*	*LIFE*	*HP*
-50	(150.45)[a]	117.80	–	61.18	N/A	72.88	204.35	(27.59)	–	0.35	(16.44)	37.28
-40	(120.22)	95.46	–	46.28	N/A	60.10	164.63	(17.42)	–	0.28	(10.72)	28.43
-30	(89.99)	72.68	–	32.87	(71.90)	46.78	124.91	(10.59)	–	0.21	(6.64)	20.43
-20	(59.76)	50.33	–	20.77	(42.22)	33.30	84.66	(5.81)	–	0.14	(3.58)	13.10
-10	(29.53)	27.56	–	9.86	(19.29)	19.00	44.62	(2.42)	–	0.07	(1.41)	6.28
0	0.00	0.00	–	0.00	0.00	0.00	0.00	0.00	0.00	0.00	0.00	0.00
10	24.86	(33.68)	–	(8.91)	19.29	(22.78)	(47.29)	1.71	–	(0.07)	0.90	(5.89)
20	44.52	(68.71)	–	(16.98)	38.59	(46.23)	(95.29)	2.90	–	(0.14)	1.43	(11.39)
30	64.17	(103.09)	–	(24.28)	57.88	(70.29)	(143.94)	3.70	(0.46)	(0.21)	1.66	(16.56)
40	83.82	(138.13)	–	(30.90)	77.17	(94.26)	N/A	4.33	–	(0.28)	1.71	(21.42)
50	103.47	(172.51)	–	(36.90)	96.46	(118.78)	–	4.84	(0.52)	(0.35)	1.56	(26.00)
60	123.12	(206.89)	–	(42.35)	115.76	(143.17)	–	5.25	–	(0.42	1.35	(30.34)
70	142.77	N/A	–	(47.30)	135.05	(168.06)	–	5.60	–	(0.49)	1.02	(34.45)
80	162.42	N/A	–	(51.80)	154.34	N/A	–	5.88	–	(0.56)	0.69	(38.37)
90	182.07	N/A	–	(55.90)	173.64	N/A	–	6.11	–	(0.64)	0.39	(42.11)
100	201.72	N/A	–	(59.63)	192.93	N/A	–	6.31	(9.67)	(0.71)	0.13	(45.68)

[a]Parentheses indicate negative values.

Table 5-17
Summary of Internal Rate of Return Percentage Changes for Twelve Variables

Percent	*EGI*	*OE*	*COST*	*r*	*REVGR*	*COUP*	*L/V*	*TERM*	*DEP*	*TRATE*	*LIFE*	*HP*
-50	(360.28)[a]	297.91	249.48	–	N/A	186.76	39.72	24.74	–	1.15	(61.41)	(21.95)
-40	(289.20)	240.42	185.37	–	N/A	155.05	36.93	19.16	–	0.90	(39.00)	(17.07)
-30	(217.42)	181.37	131.01	–	(397.21)	121.25	33.10	13.94	–	0.70	(23.76)	(12.20)
-20	(144.95)	124.74	85.02	–	(182.23)	86.06	28.22	9.06	–	0.45	(12.67)	(7.67)
-10	(71.78)	67.25	44.95	–	(72.82)	48.78	20.91	4.53	–	0.21	(5.01)	(3.83)
0	0.00	0.00	0.00	–	0.00	0.00	0.00	0.00	0.00	0.00	0.00	0.00
10	60.63	(81.88)	(45.64)	–	62.02	(59.23)	(41.81)	(4.18)	–	(0.24)	3.31	3.48
20	110.10	(166.55)	(87.80)	–	115.33	(121.95)	(120.21)	(8.36)	–	(0.49)	5.43	6.62
30	159.93	(248.78)	(125.44)	–	163.07	(187.46)	(291.64)	(12.54)	(1.39)	(0.73)	6.72	9.41
40	210.45	(331.36)	(159.23)	–	205.57	(254.01)	N/A	(16.03)	–	(0.94)	7.45	12.20
50	260.97	N/A	(189.55)	–	244.25	(323.34)	–	(18.82)	(1.79)	(1.18)	7.72	14.98
60	311.85	N/A	(216.72)	–	279.79	N/A	–	(21.60)	–	(1.43)	7.72	17.42
70	363.07	N/A	(241.81)	–	312.54	N/A	–	(23.69)	–	(1.67)	7.48	19.86
80	414.63	N/A	(264.50)	–	343.21	N/A	–	(25.44)	–	(1.88)	7.20	21.95
90	466.55	N/A	(285.37)	–	371.78	N/A	–	(26.83)	–	(2.12)	6.96	24.04
100	518.47	N/A	(304.53)	–	398.26	N/A	–	(28.22)	(34.84)	(2.37)	6.72	26.13

[a]Parentheses indicate negative values.

probably only relevant around the best guess estimate. If costs rise very quickly or suddenly, the function is very relevant and very useful.

The required rate of return, *r*, can be thought of as a function of supply and demand conditions in the market for equity capital or similar risk class. Thus ranges would exist as market conditions change, causing deviations in value and return as shown in table 5-7. Therefore, the sensitivity function for *r* is relevant not only for many deviations from the initial case but for different risk classes of investors.

The reversionary growth rate, *REVGR,* although estimated without empirical justification, can be viewed as relevant to investment decision-making at most observations in the function. With inflationary pressure increasing the nominal value of real property, many investors may prefer to invest in property for future gains as well as cash flow. Thus the growth rate in property value becomes significantly important.

The fiscal, monetary, and housing policy variables, *COUP, L/V,* and *TERM,* are easier to analyze based upon historical observation. Table 5-2 demonstrates that *COUP* has varied -20.55 to +20.83 percent from its original value. In light of the significant effect this variable can have on value or return, the sensitivity function for *COUP* is very relevant.

The loan to value ratio, *L/V*, has a small range historically (-3.37 to +3.50 percent), based upon the average ratios found in table 5-2. However, since the *L/V* ratio is a crucial variable in its effect on value and return, its sensitivity function is very relevant near the initial case and substantially less important farther away.

The length of the mortgage loan, *TERM,* has varied significantly during the past fourteen years (-6.58 to +5.88 percent). However, since *TERM* is less of a crucial variable by the results in table 5-11 and has a relatively narrow range, the theoretical sensitivities are largely immaterial.

The taxation variables include the elected depreciation method, *DEP,* the effective income tax rate, *TRATE,* the depreciable life of the improvements, *LIFE,* and the anticipated holding period, *HP*. Without exception, these variables are largely insignificant in terms of the sensitivity functions and value (or return). The allowable depreciation method, *DEP,* is not a behavioral observation but rather a behavioral response to a governmental law. Thus, it is relevant to examine the forms allowable, as long as some investors continue to consider those elections as viable alternatives.

The effective tax rate, *TRATE,* significantly varies according to the investor's income class. Although specified by law, the investor is legally bound to remit payment according to his tax bracket. To the extent that investors in many taypes of income classes consider investment in income property as a viable opportunity, the sensitivity function is relevant. It should be noted that the results found in table 5-13 indicate that there is relatively little sensitivity of changes in value or return as a result of changes in *TRATE.*

The depreciable life of apartment buildings, *LIFE,* is specified by the

Internal Revenue Service. Although this can be modified in some cases, it would appear that there is a very small range for allowable depreciable lives as of a given date. Although it is more crucial than some of the other taxation variables, most of the sensitivities are not relevant.

As previously noted, the variable holding period, *HP*, is one consideration estimated based upon presumptions and beliefs without firm empirical evidence. It can be argued that most investors really do not know how long they will maintain their interest in the property at the time of acquisition. Thus the range may extend substantially in both directions. The problem is that table 5-15 demonstrates the relatively small sensitivity of changes in value and return from changes in *HP*. Therefore, it may make little difference whether or not investors can forecast the correct holding period.

In general, for most of the variables examined, the data have shown that at most reasonable deviations from the most likely case, the possibility of the input occurring is very good. Thus, the relevance of the sensitivity function is upheld. As one moves farther and farther away, the likelihood of such an outcome becomes less likely. But for most variables, the sensitivity functions have been found to be relevant and therefore of interest in making real-world inferences.

Summary

This chapter presented the results outlined in chapter 4. After a brief discussion of each data source used for the variables in the analysis and a presentation of the typical project, the complete results have been provided in tables and graphically. While the results are the subject of chapter 6, it has been shown that each variable has a different sensitivity function and its sensitivity function can relate possible changes in its input to changes in value or return. Furthermore, it is possible to group the variables according to professional type and make some general observations as to the results. These comments are pursued in chapter 6.

A discussion reviewed the use of historical data to test the relevance of the theoretical sensitivity functions. It was found that for most of the results, ranges existed in reality indicating actual deviations from the typical case selected in this study. This result upheld the use of sensitivity functions for real-world decision-making.

Notes

1. Published as *Apartment Building Experience Exchange of Rental Income and Operating Expense Data* prior to 1966, this annual publication was retitled *Apartment Building Income-Expense Analysis* from 1966 to 1972. Beginning in 1973, it appeared with its present title, *Income-Expense Analysis.*

2. Austin J. Jaffe and C.F. Sirmans, Jr., "The Relationship Between Growth Factors, Operating Expense Ratio and Valuation in Real Estate Investment (Working Paper, University of Illinois at Urbana-Champaign, 1977).

3. Stephen E. Roulac, "Can Real Estate Outperform Common Stocks?," *Journal of Portfolio Management* 2 (Winter 1976): 26-43.

4. IPFR Publishing Corporation, *Income Property Finance Report,* vol. 1, no. 3 (New York: IPER Publishing Corp., 1977), p. 3.

5. IPFR, *Income Property Finance Report,* vol. 1, no. 5, p. 3.

6. Alan R. Winger, "Regional Growth Disparities and the Mortgage Market," *Journal of Finance* 24 (December 1969): 659-662.

7. James R. Cooper, *Real Estate Investment Analysis* (Lexington, Mass.: Lexington Books, D.C. Heath and Co., 1974), p. 114.

8. Stephen D. Messner, Irving Schreiber, and Victor L. Lyon, *Marketing Investment Real Estate* (Chicago: Realtors National Marketing Institute of the National Association of Realtors, 1975), p. 88.

9. Stephen E. Roulac, *Modern Real Estate Investment: An Institutional Approach* (San Francisco: Property Press, 1976), p. 246.

10. L.W. Ellwood, *Ellwood Tables for Real Estate Appraising and Financing* (Chicago: American Institute of Real Estate Appraisers, 1967).

11. Jack P. Friedman, "The Effect of Three Variables on the Optimal Holding Period for Income Producing Real Estate" (Ph.D. dissertation, Georgia State University, 1975).

6 Analysis of Sensitivity Functions

Introduction

This chapter serves as the forum for analysis of the findings presented in chapter 5 in light of previous work in this area. Each tested variable is discussed in dividually, by variable groups, and relative to the other variables in the study. Each finding is compared to the results reported by writers in chapter 3. A discussion also highlights some of the necessary assumptions and other limitations of using sensitivity analysis as a technique.

An important section discusses the analysis of data sensitivity in deriving sensitivity functions. This is mostly a comparative analysis of the results but the data sensitivity question is a crucial one to this study. The findings show that sensitivity analyses of this type require care when reporting the observed resulting changes based upon the input data selected but that the relative sensitivities of the outputs among sets of inputs are virtually unaffected.

This chapter then attempts to draw some implications for real estate analysts and investment modeling in light of the results. These implications will have wide-ranging effects on many disciplines and many professions. A brief summary concludes the chapter.

Analysis of Results

Each of the variables is examined in light of the results presented in chapter 5. The results are compared to those reported in the literature, originally reviewed in chapter 3. A discussion of the necessary assumptions follows the analysis.

Effective Gross Income

The *EGI* variable proved to be one of the most crucial variables in the study. Gross income was previously found to be significant by Higgins and Cunningham, Walters, Sprague, Cooper and Pyhrr, and Bleck. However, in this study, *EGI* was the most significant variable in terms of its impact on present value, except for *OE* and *L/V*, and for internal rate of return, except for *OE, REVGR,* and in some cases *L/V*. Therefore, in general, a small change in *EGI* suggests a substantial increase in value or return. The generality of this result has been verified by the data sensitivity investigation, which is discussed later.

It has been argued that net operating income (*NOI*) is a crucial figure in real estate investment analysis. *EGI* is the first number which must be maximized in order to derive a satisfactory *NOI.* In view of these results, to the extent that investors value the income stream in making investment decisions, this variable becomes critical in the decision-making process. The HUD *Survey on Tax Considerations in Multi-Family Housing Investments* found cash flow to be the most important variable for individuals, real estate groups, and real estate investment trusts (REITs).[1] Pyhrr has also stated that for lenders, the most important variables are growth rates in rents and expenses and the occupancy level.[2] While these variables have not been explicitly examined in this study, it has been suggested that changes in these variables can easily be related to changes in *EGI* and *OE* and thus similar implications would occur in terms of their sensitivity functions.

Operating Expenses

Although largely overlooked in the literature, *OE* has proven to be the most important variable in the real estate decision. Walters implied this in his *Journal of Property Management* article but most authors in investment analysis failed to concentrate on this variable. Most writers analyzed such variables as *COUP, TERM, DEP,* or *TRATE.*

The results reported here show substantial impact exerted on value and return at all intervals for *OE.* Furthermore, since the data analysis revealed a possible range for *OE,* the real-world implications are profound. *OE* appears to have been overlooked and is critical to effective decision-making.

A few writers have emphasized this result. Aldis in 1936 observed that "operating expenses are probably the most obvious indication of management efficiency."[3] He also suggested careful analysis of expenses since "even routine operating expenses" would tend to vary between different types of buildings.[4]

Hanford argued that operating expense ratios are neither permanent nor fixed by nature since "no accurate ratio exists nor will one exist in the foreseeable future."[5] He provided a number of reasons why operating expense ratios may change or why average ratios may be meaningless: identically sized buildings may have different unit mixes, inefficiencies in building design, variation in assessment practices, differences in labor costs between cities, and various leasing arrangements may result in variations in operating expenses.[6]

Hanford's conclusion about the operating expense ratio is a simple one: generalizations are very limited if applicable at all. An analysis of each project's expense ratio is the only accurate way of carefully researching the effect of operating expenses. This requires a proposed management plan.[7]

This study has therefore shown that changes in operating expenses are very important in terms of their potential impact on value and return. In the view of a small but growing minority of writers, *OE* is a very critical input. The result drawn from this analysis is that although overlooked by most real estate analysts historically, *OE* is a variable which must be considered as important or more so than all others. Since the property manager is best able to do this and implement changes, his role in the investment decision-making process becomes crucial to successful ventures.

Costs of Acquisition

The variable *COST* proved to be a highly significant one in the analysis. While it is not needed as an input in the calculation of present value, it varied more than any of the other variables in the internal rate of return calculation, with the exception of *EGI, OE,* and *REVGR.* It was calculated on the basis of per square foot costs and thus varied according to hypothetical changes in construction costs. In the internal rate of return calculation, it represented the present value acquisition cost, hypothetically available in the market.

A few writers have suggested *COST* as a crucial variable. Gallagher, Walters, Bleck, and Hemmer reported results for *COST.* However, a recent survey by Wiley reported that only 10 percent of all investors were concerned with the purchase price.[8] He reported that investors tended to emphasize return on equity and cash flows. While it is clear that the purchase price will affect return on equity and most likely is affected by expected cash flows, given the results presented here, one might think investors would tend to become more concerned about the acquisition cost of potential investments. In any case, it has been shown that changes in this variable have a relatively strong impact on return.

Required Rate of Return

The required rate of return (*r*), or equity yield, was found to have only a moderate impact on value when changed from the initial case. However, the results are substantial relative to those found in many of the other variables. In addition, the results of the data sensitivity test show that as the typical project becomes a more favorable project, the variable becomes even less significant. Thus for marginal projects, the required rate of return must be considered important: but as the project becomes more favorable, changes in this variable become less significant.

Gibbons argued that the overall rate of capitalization, of which *r* is a part, "is the *key* to the valuation process."[9] The results of this study showed that although *r* is a variable that is important relative to many others, it is doubtful whether its impact on yield warrants the attention it has received. One preliminary implication is that the estimate of the required rate of return is less crucial than most have thought, relative to other more important variables.

Reversion Growth Rate

The interest in the property that is sold at the end of the holding period may be higher or lower than the original buying price. Whether this change will be positive or negative will theoretically depend upon whether the discounted present value of future after-tax cash flows after the time of sale is higher or lower than the original selling price. This in turn is thought to be a function of many things which generally include owner's objectives, maintenance programs, local market conditions, and governmental tax policies. One way to account for different possibilities is to introduce growth rates into the calculation of the reversionary interest.

This study found that the degree of growth expected in the future selling price is a more important consideration than has typically been believed. For the case selected, expected percentage growth rates in reversion growth rate (*REVGR*) have almost as much impact on value (and slightly less on return) as do changes in *EGI*. This result, while generally not startling, even if typically overlooked, might explain why investors in recent years have tended to value income property highly, although cash flows have been remarkably low, due largely to rising operating costs. If this suggestion proves true, the result derived in this study will provide better justification and understanding of this process.

On the other hand, the National Institute of Farm and Land Brokers has emphasized the future selling price. Stating that the expected selling price assumption is the most critical, they warned that failure to thoroughly understand the effect of sales price can "materially affect the computed overall rate of return on a particular investment."[10] Therefore, the results reported here have upheld this general warning, and suggest that a very careful analysis of *REVGR* can be extremely useful.

Interest Rate on Mortgage

The stated rate of interest (*COUP*) has shown to be a moderate variable in the sensitivity analysis. However, with the unfavorable project used in this analysis, increases in *coup* drastically reduced the internal rate of return. At a 50 percent increase, the internal rate of return fell to -6.4 percent (an enormous 323 percent change). However, with a more favorable project, *COUP* showed more modest but significant changes (See tables A-14 and A-15). Walters' results found the interest rate on the mortgage to be significantly important as well. However, in this study, relative to other results, *COUP* showed only a slightly better than average impact on value and return.

Boeckmann has emphasized the alleged dramatic impact on real estate that rising mortgage money would have for property.[11] Although his argument is weak, others have suggested similar implications that result from restrictive regulations on financial institutions and loan arrangements, which raise the effective cost of borrowing. When interest rate levels rise, a diminished supply of available funds would substantially raise the "costs" of borrowing and thus, make this variable important. However, in terms of the sensitivities derived in this study, the results suggest only an average sensitivity function for the variable *COUP* in most cases.

Loan to Value Ratio

As table 3-7 suggested, the loan to value or *L/V* ratio was one of the variables emphasized most often in the literature. This study confirms previous investigations that the *L/V* ratio is an important variable. Using both sets of data, this study showed that sensitivity of present values to changes in *L/V* is much greater than the sensitivity of internal rates of return to similar changes in *L/V*. For present values, it is one of the most important variables considered. For internal rates of return, it is highly significant, although more moderate.

One point ought to be made regarding *L/V*. Changes in the *L/V* ratio relate directly to changes in the amount of equity supplied. Sensitivity analysis assumes independence of the many variables in order to compute these reported changes. In this case, it seems highly questionable as to whether the interest rates or the length of the mortgage period associated with different *L/V* ratios are constant. Therefore, the reader is cautioned about these results. The answer to this problem may be the subject of future research.

Length of the Mortgage

Walters found a relatively small impact on return for this variable (*TERM*). The results of this study largely confirm his findings. Since the project is a relatively unattractive one, the effect of negative leverage can be seen in the results of the actual rate of return. For this project, the longer the *TERM*, the more adversely affected is the return on the project. By comparison, using the favorable project in table A-15, possible increases in *TERM* exert a positive influence on return.

Using the original data in this study, there are only three or four variables that are less crucial in terms of their sensitivity functions: *DEP, TRATE, LIFE,* and possibly *HP*. As a result, *TERM,* which has generally been regarded as a significant if not critical variable in terms of sensitivities, has been shown to be much less important in terms of analyzing real estate projects. In other words, this study has shown that the decision for the length of period of the loan for interests in real property is a relatively unimportant one. The impact of any of the *TERM* values is relatively small.

Depreciation Method

As noted earlier, the depreciation method (*DEP*) elected is one of the set of methods allowable by law, dependent upon the type and age of the property and the legal status of the owner. Many writers and accountants have argued that the proper depreciation method election is one of the most crucial decisions an investor must make. This study has conclusively shown that with the exception of the method of double-declining balance, the relative impact on favorable or unfavorable projects is very insignificant.

While it is no doubt clear that depreciation writeoffs are one of the biggest attractions for equity capital in real estate, these results imply that changes from straight-line depreciation to accelerated methods have smaller impacts than many may suspect. While it is true, as Martin suggests, that "a property's cash flow is increased substantially by the depreciation write-off provision,"[12] changes in the rate of depreciation have been shown to have minimal effects. Edwards and Goodwin examined the benefits of the 125 percent declining balance method and concluded that the likelihood of benefits to the user was small and that "little harm would be done if [the method] were eliminated."[13] Walters concluded that depreciation methods have relatively little impact on valuation as well.

However, the HUD study found that 77 percent of all investors used accelerated depreciation. [This seems reasonable since the sensitivity results showed positive (negative) impacts on return and value for favorable (unfavorable) projects.] But the study also reported "most investors believe that depreciation is the *key tax element* contributing to the overall economic return from an investment in an apartment project" (italics supplied).[14] The National Institute of Farm and Land Brokers stated that "one of the most useful planning techniques in real estate investment is the use of depreciation as a tax shelter."[15]

In light of the results reported in this study, these beliefs in the use of accelerated depreciation and the expected benefits to be derived are largely unfounded after more careful analysis and an examination of depreciation in the equity valuation equation.

Investor's Tax Rate

Much has been written dealing with the impact that income taxes (investors tax rate or *TRATE*) have on value, return, risk, incentive, and theoretical developments in real estate and other applied economic disciplines. Most writers concluded that tax considerations are a relevant and important concern. Analysis of a problem without consideration of taxes is a crude or preliminary endeavor at best.

This study has not examined the impact that taxes have on property. It has been assumed that it is substantial and one which must be considered. This study has concerned itself with what effect changes in taxes will have on valuation. The answer is conclusively very little. Tables 5-16 and 5-17 show minimal changes in value and return as a result of large changes in tax rates. (The results of the data sensitivity study show slightly larger results.) Therefore, while taxes are important in real estate investment analysis, changes in tax rates and thus tax liability have been shown to be relatively unimportant.

Since "many investors believe that changes in the tax law could be most effective in increasing the return,"[16] it would be fair to suggest that investors feel *TRATE* would be a crucial variable and thus return and value would be sensitive to changes in *TRATE*. This study has shown that the opposite is true; *TRATE* is one of the most insignificant varialbles in terms of sensitivity analysis and thus its importance with respect to changes or errors in estimating it is only a minor concern.

Depreciable Life of Assets

The results showed that changes in the depreciable life of the real assets (*LIFE*) would have very minor effects on return and value. The study has also shown that dependent upon the attractiveness of the project, changes in *LIFE* will either increase or decrease return and value. In any case, the effect is relatively small.

It is not surprising, though, that the HUD study reported many investors would favor shorter depreciable lives if allowable and tax change would be an effective method "to draw more investors to apartment investments."[17] While the results indicate that as long as the project is favorable, returns and values will increase with shorter depreciable periods, the magnitudes of the possible changes are very small. If, using the extreme case, apartment buildings were allowed to be depreciated over 50 percent fewer years than the current forty-year period, return would only increase by 5.18 percent. Thus belief in this method as a major tax incentive is largely a myth.

Holding Period

The optimal holding period (*HP*) may be defined as that period which maximizes the present value or internal rate of return, or both. Much recent interest has been generated in attempting to determine the optimal holding period. Messner and Findlay's FMRR can be used in this sense.[18] Wiley's survey reports holding periods for investors: 11 percent sold after five years, 32 percent after ten years, 15 percent after twenty years, and 42 percent at various other times.[19] Friedman examined whether depreciation methods, depreciable life, or amortization term affected the optimal holding period.[20] In general, he found these variables had little or no effect on the optimal holding period.

This study, however, has found that when investors sell their property or which variables affect the return based upon the date they sell the property are relatively unimportant and thus less interesting questions than many others. The results indicate that the holding period concern is a relatively unimportant one, especially if the project is a favorable one. Thus an analyst would be better off analyzing crucial variables than worrying about the optimal time to sell. The results here indicate that the rewards of such endeavors are very, very small.

The HUD study reported that most investors stated that they did not have a specific holding period in mind at the time of acquisition.[21] This was most likely because there has not been any proof, in any general framework, of how long an investor should hold onto the property. In light of these results, those investors most likely risked very little. This evidence suggests that although optimal holding periods are determinable, they appear to be relatively unimportant.

Presumptions and Limitations

These reported results were based upon a number of presumptions and limitations. Perhaps the major one is that the basis of the technique of sensitivity analysis rests upon the ceteris paribus condition so often used in economics and finance. All of the reported results and ensuing implications are based upon changes in the variable under study, all else being the same. Under this assumption, the sensitivity analysis reports how the result changes as a result of a change in the initial variable. To the extent that the variables are not independent of one another, this assumption tends to be more and more restrictive. If two or more variables were known to be dependent upon one another, the sensitivity analysis should be done using this relationship in the test. Since these relationships are generally not known precisely, they are presumed to be independent and the results reported as such.

Another presumption is the belief that investors are using the criteria of discounted present values or internal rates of return. The HUD survey reported that only 2 percent of the passive investors and only 4 percent of the active investors used discounted cash flow criteria for measuring profitability.[22] It has been shown that these measures are superior to other criteria which fail to adjust for time, taxes, or reversion. Therefore, the results of this study are meaningful only to those investors who use similar criteria.

It has also been assumed that investors are interested in maximizing their economic well-being, that is, maximizing net present value or internal rate of return. If an investor is operating under an alternative objective function, these results may not be meaningful to him. In general, these results are directed to profit-oriented investors whether they think they would value cash flow, tax shelter benefits, liquidity, capital appreciation, financial leverage, fees from packaging, or pride of ownership. These factors are irrelevant to the findings of this study. These goals may not be irrelevant to prospective investors, but that is a different concern.

Finally, the question of the sensitivity of data selection for the analysis is important. Are the results derived here general enough to include many projects with similar characteristics, values, or returns? Are these results applicable to other types of apartment buildings or other property types as well? Are these conclusions and the implications from them general enough to be used as tools in real estate investment analysis or simply on a case-by-case basis? The answers to these questions are in the next section.

Analysis of Data Sensitive Problems

An important aspect of this study is a determination of the generality of the sensitivity analysis results. If the results were to vary for each set of data inputs (that is, for each investment), the generality of the results would be nonexistent and much of the effort of this study would be futile. However, if some or most of the results can be shown to be true for various sets of data, generalizations may be drawn from the results presented here and sensitivity analysis as a technique may be viewed as a method of investigating the importance of various variables on value and return, regardless of the data used. The results reported in this section using the values generated in this study strongly suggest that these results are not very data sensitive and that the generalizations and conclusions may be useful for many types of real estate projects with many types of financial and physical characteristics.

The type of analysis for data sensitivity described in this regard can be easily accomplished by varying the initial parameter inputs and comparing the percentage change results (or the relative rankings of importance) in both sets of data. If the results of this procedure indicate major differences between the sets of results, the results, implications, and generalizations of the study will be data sensitive. However, if the use of different data sets proves not to substantially alter the results, data sensitivity can be assumed to pose no threat to the study.

Table 6-1 presents typical rankings of the variables examined in this study. The present value and internal rate of return results of series II can be found in the appendix. They are summarized in tables A-14 and A-15.

The answers to the data sensitivity questions may be summarized by the following observations: in general, the percentage changes reported for each variable will tend to vary, according to the original data set, but the rankings of relative importance of the resulting percentage changes will, with few exceptions, remain constant. Furthermore, although these rankings are not identical for the present value series and the internal rate of return series, they are very similar when classified according to variable group. Finally, this analysis has shown that the rankings of relative importance are comparatively more similar between decision criteria (present value series versus the internal rate of return series) than they are for the data sets (series I versus series II) for the crucial variables. For the less crucial variables, the rankings are more alike according to data set.

Therefore, it appears that data sensitivity is a relatively minor concern in terms of the conclusions of this study. However, it has been shown that reliance upon the percentage change series per se is very data sensitive and thus the specific results cannot be used beyond the project under study. But since the rankings remain constant with various sets of data, the user can be assured of the results of this study that specify the significant and insignificant variables in terms of their impact on the criteria.

Table 6-1
Typical Rankings of Importance of Variables by Series and Criterion

VAR	*PV I*	*PV II*	*IRR I*	*IRR II*
EGI	3	3	3	2
OE	2	2	1	1
COST	–	–	5	5
r	6	6	–	–
REVGR	4	4	2	3
COUP	5	5	4	6
L/V	1	1	6	4
TERM	8	8	7	7.5
DEP	10	9	10	9
TRATE	11	7	11	7.5
LIFE	9	10	8	10
HP	7	11	9	11

In conclusion, it has been shown that data sensitivity becomes a concern when the user wishes to analyze the precise sensitivity of value or return to changes in his variables. If this is desired, a sensitivity analysis should be performed. However, if an investor would like to know which variables are more crucial than others in influencing yield or value, the results reported here can be used to answer his questions.

Implications for Real Estate Investment

Many implications arise from the results of this study. First and foremost, it is now apparent, subject to the limitations and assumptions, that within the framework of analysis used here, which variables are crucial as evidenced by their sensitivity functions in terms of their impact on value or return. Since this study has shown that certain variables are more significant than others, users can now: (1) measure the sensitivity of variables in questions using Whisler's method or a complete sensitivity approach, with the knowledge of the relative sensitivity that variable has in the equity valuation function; and (2) better understand and interpret the importance of the variable in the equity valuation function and thus respond accordingly.

One of the major implications is the educational benefits that users of these results will have in terms of understanding the relationship of these twelve variables to real estate values and yields. Based upon the inconclusive consensus of opinion reported in chapter 3, many writers have regarded many insignificant variables as significant, or vice versa. Some analysts overlooked important concerns; others overemphasized some variables. This research may help to clear up the divergence of opinion as to the sensitivity functions of these variables.

Another implication of these results is that investors can now make use of these findings in terms of seeking professional advice and services from those that can aid them in maximizing profits. Those professionals who can help alter the variables that have been shown to be crucial may tend to be more valuable to the investor than those who cannot provide the same services. Thus, as suggested by Walters, the allocation of dollars for professional services ought to reflect this consideration. One would most likely be interested in trying to improve those items that affect value (or return) rather than those that fail to have an effect.

Finally, the results presented here suggest a reevaluation of real estate investment analysis. While traditionally property management has been either excluded as a professional input into the decision process or has been degraded to the back room, these results imply that the importance of effective property management cannot be overstated. Furthermore, the emphasis on accounting and taxation variables in the literature has led much of the profession to evaluate real estate in terms of depreciation methodology, tax rates, depreciable bases, and holding period analysis. These results suggest that based upon the relative insensitivity that value and return have to changes in these variables, the attention that has traditionally been paid to these considerations is largely unnecessary. This reevaluation would shift attention and interest from those variables that are not crucial to effective decision-making to those that are crucial. Since real estate decision-making involves an allocation of time, effort, and money, this new direction is an essential step.

Therefore, based upon the results of this study, it is hoped that the methodology of real estate decision-making and thus real estate valuation can reassess its position and reexamine much of the traditional doctrine. Also, this study has perhaps proven to be a positive addition to the literature in that it has emphasized which changes in variables are important rather than which changes in variables are relatively unimportant.

Summary

This chapter has provided the necessary analysis of the results derived in chapter 5. It has shown that changes in the property management variables (effective gross income, *EGI*, and operating expenses, *OE*) are the most important variables in terms of their impact on value and return. The results also showed that the loan to value ratio (*L/V*) and the reversion growth rate changes (*REVGR*) were relatively more important than had previously been suggested.

The other purchase and sale variables (construction cost, *COST*, and required rate of return, *r*) and the other monetary, fiscal, and housing policy variables (mortgage interest rate, *COUP*, and length of the mortgage, *LIFE*) were shown to have moderate impacts on valuation and yield when varied in the analysis. Changes in the taxation or accounting variables (depreciation method, *DEP*; effective tax rate, *TRATE*; depreciable life, *LIFE*; and holding period, *HP*) were shown to be relatively unimportant and insignificant.

A brief discussion of the limitations and assumptions necessary in sensitivity analysis suggested that independence, matching criteria, identical goals, and data sensitivity presumptions are necessary for an analysis of this type. The analysis of whether the results were based upon the magnitude of the parameters or were general for all sets of data followed. It was shown that the relative sensitivities are constant for all data sets but the individual percentage changes were based upon the input parameters only.

A brief discussion of the implications of these findings concluded the chapter. These included a better knowledge of the valuation equation and its relevance to selecting professional services and other educational benefits, and suggest a reevaluation of real estate investment analysis.

Notes

1. Arnold H. Diamond, "Motivations of Investors in Multifamily Housing," *The Real Estate Appraiser* 38 (May/June 1972): 17.

2. Stephen A. Pyhrr, "Analytical Methods Can Reduce Income Property Loan Losses," *The Real Estate Appraiser* 41 (March/April 1975): 39.

3. Graham Aldis, "Management as a Factor in Appraisal," *The Appraisal Journal* 4 (April 1936): 189.

4. Ibid., p. 190.

5. Lloyd D. Hanford, Jr., "Expense Ratios and Their Use," *The Appraisal Journal* 41 (January 1973): 100.

6. Ibid., p. 101.

7. Ibid., p. 102.

8. Robert J. Wiley, "Real Estate Investment Analysis: An Empirical Study," *The Appraisal Journal* 44 (October 1976): 588.

9. James E. Gibbons, "Impact of Yields on Value," *The Appraisal Journal* 38 (October 1970): 509.

10. National Institute of Farm and Land Brokers, *Federal Taxes Affecting Real Estate,* rev. ed. (Chicago: National Institute of Farm and Land Brokers of the National Institute of Real Estate Brokers, 1970), pp. 340-341.

11. Henry J. Boeckmann, "The High Cost of Money and Its Effect on Real Estate Valuations," *The Appraisal Journal* 43 (October 1975): 579.

12. Wendell H. Martin, "Tax Shelter and the Real Estate Analyst," *The Appraisal Journal* 43 (January 1975): 17.

13. Charles E. Edwards and Jack S. Goodwin, "An Evaluation of Tax Shields from Declining Balance Depreciation at 1.25% Times the Straight-Line Rate," *The Appraisal Journal* 43 (October 1975): 53.

14. U.S. Department of Housing and Urban Development, *Study on Tax Considerations in Multi-Family Housing Investments,* HUD contract H-1227, May 7, 1971, p. 10.

15. National Institute of Farm and Land Brokers, *Federal Taxes*

16. HUD, *Study on Tax Considerations,* p. 10.

17. Ibid., p. 11.

18. Stephen D. Messner and M. Chapman Findlay, III, "Real Estate Investment Analysis" p. 17.

19. Wiley, "Real Estate Investment Analysis," p. 592.

20. Jack P. Friedman, "The Effect of Three Variables on the Optimal Holding Period for Income-Producing Real Estate," (Ph.D. dissertation, Georgia State University, 1975).

21. HUD, *Study on Tax Considerations,* p. 9.

22. Diamond, "Motivations of Investors," p. 19.

7 Summary and Conclusions

Summary of Findings

The following is a summary of the major findings in this study.

1. A review of the traditional real estate investment literature has found that prior to the middle 1960s, this field lacked a developed methodology for evaluating real estate investment property. Many major theoretical advancements and the development of computerized valuation models in the early 1970s have apparently filled much of the gap in expertise, knowledge, and methods. In addition, the literature of financial decision-making has provided new ideas and answers to previously unsolved problems of real estate analysts.

2. It has been observed that one of the deficiencies in the state of the art of real estate modeling has been the lack of understanding of concepts and techniques of modeling, theory building, and decision science. This study reviewed many of the developments in management science and operations research in the area of decision-making to provide a better basis for understanding many of the tools used by real estate analysts, apparently with little or no comprehension. Furthermore, the review may well provide the missing link between decision analysis, scientific decision-making, and real estate investment analysis.

3. A review of the sensitivity studies in the literature showed that a lack of agreement exists among writers regarding the importance of variables in real estate valuation. In general, a majority of the authors tended to focus upon those variables that are relatively insignificant in terms of their impact on yield, while only a few examined the crucial variables. In the case of operating expenses, this study found it to be the most crucial of all the variables in terms of its impact on yield and value, although most writers tended to overlook it. It has also been shown that the relative importance of the variable in terms of valuation remained unknown to the consensus of writers. This study may provide answers to this unsettled area of analysis.

4. After a general discussion of the features and limitations of the equity valuation model, this study respecified the model and examined the general changes in the model as a result of changes in many of its variables. These results, using differential calculus, could have been used to complete the study but were rejected in favor of computerization. However, the completely specified model was shown to be a relatively complex function.

5. The theoretical development of the technique of sensitivity analysis was

critically reviewed and analyzed. The most recent development by Whisler provided a sound method of analyzing sensitivities to cash flow changes. While this was shown to be an advancement and a helpful approach, its usefulness is unclear due to its lack of generality and overall complexity. Furthermore, the complete sensitivity analysis performed in this study is more general and more conclusive.

6. After specifying the parameters for a testing of the importance of property management hypothesis by Walters, sensitivity functions were derived for a typical multiple-family income property. Input parameters and initial variable values were determined by a brief data analysis in order to derive the typical project, with some concern for empirical results. Based upon this analysis, the typical project was a relatively unattractive one, yielding only 2.87 percent. The results are presented in tables and graphical form.

7. A discussion of the relevance of behavioral data analysis addressed the question of the relevance of theoretical sensitivities to real-world decision-making. The analysis concluded that based upon historical data, nearly all of the variables had moderate to substantial variations over time, and therefore the importance of potential changes in the variables was relevant.

8. The study showed that by using sensitivity analysis, one can identify the crucial and the insignificant variables. In general, this study found that changes in the property management variables exert the most significant impacts in terms of their sensitivity functions; changes in the purchase and sale variables and changes in fiscal, monetary, and housing policy variables have more moderate effects on return and value; and changes in the taxation variables are relatively insignificant in terms of sensitivity. Based upon the literature and apparent beliefs of many writers, this result appears to be contradictory and counterintuitive. However, the conclusiveness of the findings and the lack of data sensitivity to relative rankings confirm the suspicion that the relative sensitivities of these variables have remained largely unknown.

9. Of the two property management variables, changes in operating expenses proved to be more important. This finding appears to be important in that if these variables were examined at all, effective gross income was most likely examined. In fact, most of the literature failed to focus on operating expenses, although it is the most crucial variable.

10. The cost of acquiring the property and the expected growth rate in the reversion were found to be more significant than has generally been assumed. Changes in the required rate of return tended to be overemphasized in light of the findings in this study. In general, changes in the purchase and sale variables were significant, and thus should be regarded in that sense. Also, the required rate of return decreased in significance as the project became more favorable.

11. The loan to value ratio was shown to be an important variable, as much of the literature had suggested. For the present value calculations, this

variable was the most crucial in terms of its sensitivity. Thus this result confirms the fact that leverage is an important factor in real estate analysis.

12. Changes in the interest rate on the mortgage were found to have only an average impact on return and value. Although this variable is thought to be crucial by many observers, the results confirmed the suspicion that its importance has most likely been overstated.

13. The length of the mortgage was shown to be relatively insignificant in terms of the input changes this variable had on valuation. Although the effect is related to the attractiveness of the investment project, the relative impact is very small. In general, the decision of the length of the borrowing period for long-term mortgages is a relatively unimportant one.

14. Changes in the taxation variables resulted in only minimal changes in return or value. Most significant was the effective tax rate, although its effect was only marginally more significant than the depreciable life of the improvements, the depreciation method, or the expected holding period.

15. The election of the allowable depreciation method proved to be a relatively unimportant decision. Although the double-declining method was found to have some impact, the less accelerated methods added little to value or return. This finding is important due to the relative importance given to depreciation allowances for real estate as a policy variable by the federal legislature.

16. Changes in the tax rate had small effects on value. Although this variable has traditionally been regarded as significant, this study showed that as a result of the insensitivity of value and return to changes in the tax rate, the interest in this variable has been overstated.

17. The depreciable life of assets was another relatively unimportant variable. Although generally believed to be important and apparently used in tax policy, changes in this variable will not significantly affect value or yield.

18. The holding period was a relatively insignificant variable. Recent attempts to identify, measure, and analyze the optimal holding periods for real estate projects, in light of these findings, largely become futile exercises. As noted earlier, the rewards of these attempts apparently are very small.

19. These results are based upon some presumptions that are relatively restrictive. Each of the variables is assumed to be independent of one another, and thus changes in any of the variables would occur without changes in other values. It is suspected that this assumption is a severe one. In addition, it is assumed that investors use discounted cash flow criteria and profit maximization as a goal in evaluating real estate. The results are a function of the data used in the valuation process, although data sensitivity was not a major problem.

20. The results were found to be data sensitive in terms of their precise impacts on value and return. In other words, the impact that changes in one variable would have on value and return will vary dependent upon the set of input parameters used. However, the relative rankings of the importance of the variables has been shown to remain relatively constant for various data sets.

Therefore, for purposes of identifying crucial variables, data sensitivity is not a problem or constraint. To identify the sensitivity of value and return to changes in a certain variable, a case-by-case analysis must be made.

21. These results implied that users have not fully understood the equity valuation model. As long as analysts continue to expend resources on insignificant variables and bypass crucial variables, potential hazards for effective investment decisions may ensue.

22. Finally, this study has confirmed Walters' importance of property management hypothesis to a large extent by confirming his findings more completely, and by generalizing his preliminary results.

Conclusions

Since the appearance of Walters' article in the *Journal of Property Management* in 1973, little recognition or attention has been made of his preliminary findings. This study tested the hypothesis proposed in that paper by examining generally and more completely the relationships various variables have among themselves, and concluded that Walters' importance of property management hypothesis has been upheld, based upon the results.

Although Walters found gross income to be the most important variable and the interest rate to be slightly more important than was found here, the general breakdown of variables follows almost without flaw. His startling conclusions can now be backed up with more substantiated and extensive analysis.

Walters' conclusions emphasized the importance of the property manager for the investor interested in maximizing return. This study's results not only emphasize this fact but present additional evidence of the importance of property management to investment decision-making. It is the professional property manager who is most likely to increase rates of return on marginal projects, devise innovative alterations to make unattractive property profitable, and cut unnecessary costs, since he is trained and can judge best when such changes should be made.

The traditional role of the property manager as rent collector or management departments as loss leaders for sales is rapidly becoming obsolete. As rising expenses continue to plague owners and profitability becomes more and more elusive, those who hire the services of professional management will acquire the expertise and informed advice necessary to help in problem situations. This study has confirmed prior beliefs in the importance of a well-trained manager in the investment decision. In the future, he may be the most valuable member of the team.

Suggestions for Further Research

There are a number of extensions and recommendations for further research in this area of study. One major area of investigation is an examination of the usefulness of Whisler's method of sensitivity analysis. A number of questions need to be answered if this development can be useful in real-world decision-making. For example, can the method be used for variables that do not affect cash flow but affect value or return? Is the method operational enough to be able to incorporate it into the decision-making process, as has been suggested by decision theory writers? Is this method or any sensitivity analysis approach general enough to be used for all types of property at various times in the life cycle of the real estate project?

Another suggestion would be to investigate the interdependence among variables. If the input variables are not independent, as many have suggested, what is the relationship between them? Furthermore, even if we estimate the relationships between the variables using ex post data, can we use these results for our ex ante predictions? In other words, can we use this economic model with some degree of reliability and stationariness for future investment decision-making?

It would also be valuable to derive measures or values for the degree of data sensitivity present in sensitivity analyses. Although this concern was shown to be relatively small in this study, it would be helpful if the analyst could know the sensitivity of his percentage changes. This study showed that these percentage changes vary with the data inputs. Further analysis might shed light on this observation, and perhaps explain the underlying reasons for the results and how to interpret them.

Alternative techniques might be used to verify or refute the results derived in this sensitivity analysis. Factor analysis, for example, might be applied to real estate data in an attempt to measure the contributions of various variables to value. Another development might be a decision analysis approach to real estate valuation rather than a discounted cash flow valuation function, whether deterministic or probabilistic in design. Alternative investment criteria could be examined, such as the FMRR, with regard to sensitivity measures.

A further implication of these results might suggest the importance of decision-making variables for other types of analysis. For example, do the results of this sensitivity analysis imply a redirection for feasibility analysis? Can a better understanding of the impact of various variables help in aiding development and location decisions?

Finally, a most useful development would be a general methodology for analyzing and identifying sensitivities between variables, given that the interdependencies of the variables are known. This would improve the results found in this study by identifying the sensitivities of value and return to changes in input variables based upon some theoretical relationship between the variables. Once these relationships were known, it would be useful to have a method of computing the sensitivities of potential changes in the variables in light of the economic relationships. In a sense, this is an improvement of this study to a large extent in that the results would be directly applicable to future decision-making since they would be based upon theoretically tested interdependencies. It is hoped that this study will push one step closer to that goal.

Bibliography

Books

Babcock, Frederick M. *The Valuation of Real Estate.* New York: McGraw-Hill Book Company, 1932.

Barton, Richard F. *A Primer on Simulation and Gaming.* Englewood Cliffs, N.J.: Prentice-Hall, 1970.

Baumol, William J. *Economic Theory and Operations Analysis.* 3d ed. Englewood Cliffs, N.J.: Prentice-Hall, 1972.

Beaton, William R. *Real Estate Investment.* Englewood Cliffs, N.J.: Prentice-Hall, 1971.

Beaton, William R., and Robertson, Terry. *Real Estate Investment.* 2d ed. Englewood Cliffs, N.J.: Prentice-Hall, 1977.

Bierman, Harold; Bonini, Charles P.; and Hausman, Warren H. *Quantitative Analysis for Business Decisions.* 4th ed. Homewood, Ill.: Richard D, Irwin, 1973.

Bierman, Harold, and Smidt, Seymour. *The Capital Budgeting Decision.* 3d ed. New York: Macmillan Company, 1971.

Boot, John C.G. *Mathematical Reasoning in Economics and Management Science.* Englewood Cliffs, N.J.: Prentice-Hall, 1967.

Bridge, J., and Dodds, J.C. *Managerial Decision Making.* New York: John Wiley and Sons, 1975.

Carter, L.R., and Hazan, E. *A Practical Approach to Computer Simulation in Business.* New York: John Wiley and Sons, 1973.

Cerf, Alan R. *Real Estate and the Federal Income Tax.* Englewood Cliffs, N.J.: Prentice-Hall, 1965.

Chacko, George K. *Computer-Aided Decision-Making.* New York: American Elsevier Publishing Co., 1972.

Chorafas, D.N. *Systems and Simulation.* New York: Academic Press, 1965.

Cooper, James R. *Real Estate Investment Analysis.* Lexington, Mass.: Lexington Books, D.C. Heath and Company, 1974.

Crecine, John P. *Governmental Problem-Solving.* Chicago: Rand McNally and Company, 1969.

Durbin, Robert, *Theory Building.* New York: Free Press, 1969.

Ebert, Ronald J., and Mitchell, Terence R. *Organizational Decision Processes.* New York: Crane, Russak and Company, 1975.

Emshoff, James R., and Sisson, Roger L. *Decision and Use of Computer Simulation Models.* New York: Macmillan Company, 1970.

Ferber, Robert, and Verdoun, P.J. *Research Methods in Economics and Business.* New York: Macmillan Company, 1962.

Francis, Jack Clark, and Archer, Stephen H. *Portfolio Analysis.* Englewood Cliffs, N.J.: Prentice-Hall, 1971.

Gordon, Geoffrey. *System Simulation.* Englewood Cliffs, N.J.: Prentice-Hall, 1969.

Grayson, C. Jackson, Jr. *Decisions Under Uncertainty: Drilling by Oil and Gas Operators.* Boston: Division of Research, Harvard Business School, 1960.

Grebler, Leo. *Experience in Urban Real Estate Investment.* New York: Columbia University Press, 1955.

Hanssmann, Fred. *Operations Research Techniques for Capital Investment.* New York: John Wiley and Sons, 1968.

Harrison, E. Frank. *The Managerial Decision-Making Process.* Boston: Houghton-Mifflin Company, 1975.

Harrison, Ian W. *Capital Investment Appraisal.* London: McGraw-Hill Book Company, 1973.

Hillier, Frederick S., and Lieberman, Gerald J. *Introduction to Operations Research.* San Francisco: Holden-Day, 1967.

Horowitz, Ira. *An Introduction to Quantitative Business Analysis.* 2d ed. New York: McGraw-Hill Book Company, 1972.

Jones, G.T. *Simulation and Business Decisions.* Middlesex, England: Penguin Books, 1972.

Kahn, Sanders A.; Case, Frederick E.; and Schimmel, Alfred. *Real Estate Appraisal and Investment,* New York: Ronald Press, 1963.

Kinnard, William N., Jr. *Income Property Valuation.* Lexington, Mass.: Lexington Books, D.C. Heath and Company, 1971.

Knight, Frank H. *Risk, Uncertainty and Profit.* Boston: Houghton-Mifflin Company, 1923.

Luce, R.D., and Raiffa, Howard. *Games and Decisions: Introduction and Critical Survey.* New York: John Wiley and Sons, 1957.

Maisel, Sherman J., and Roulac, Stephen E. *Real Estate Investment and Finance.* New York: McGraw-Hill Book Company, 1976.

Mao, James C.T. *Quantitative Analysis of Financial Decisions.* New York: Macmillan Company, 1969.

McMahan, John. *Property Development–Effective Decision Making in Uncertain Times.* New York: McGraw-Hill Book Company, 1976.

McMillan, Claude, and Gonzalez, Richard F. *Systems Analysis.* 3d ed. Homewood, Ill.: Richard D. Irwin, 1973.

Meier, Robert C.; Newell, William T.; and Payer, Harold L. *Simulation in Business and Economics.* Englewood Cliffs, N.J.: Prentice-Hall, 1969.

Messner, Stephen D.; Schreiber, Irving; and Lyon, Victor L. *Marketing Investment Real Estate.* Chicago: Realtors National Marketing Institute of the National Association of Realtors, 1975.

Mize, Joe H., and Cox, J. Grady. *Essentials of Simulation.* Englewood Cliffs, N.J.: Prentice-Hall, 1968.

Naylor, Thomas H., ed. *The Design of Computer Simulation Experiments.* Durham, N.C.: Duke University Press, 1969.

Naylor, Thomas H.; Balintfy, Joseph L.; Burdick, Donald S.; and Chu, King. *Computer Simulation Techniques.* New York: John Wiley and Sons, 1966.

Paranka, Stephen. *Business Applications of Decision Sciences.* New York: Petrocelli/Charter Publishers, 1975.

Pouliquen, Louis Y. *Risk Analysis in Project Appraisal.* Baltimore, Md.: Johns Hopkins Press, 1970.

Quirin, G. David. *The Capital Expenditure Decision.* Homewood, Ill.: Richard D. Irwin, 1967.

Raiffa, Howard. *Decision Analysis–Introductory Lectures on Choices Under Uncertainty.* Menlo Park: Addison Wesley, 1968.

Raiffa, Howard, and Schlaifer, Robert O. *Applied Statistical Decision Theory.* New York: McGraw-Hill Book Company, 1968.

Ratcliff, Richard U. *Real Estate Analysis.* New York: McGraw-Hill Book Company, 1961.

Richmond, Samuel B. *Operations Research for Management Decisions.* New York: Ronald Press Company, 1968.

Rigby, Paul H. *Models in Business Analysis.* Columbus, Ohio: Charles E. Merrill Publishing Co., 1969.

Riggs, James L., and Inoue, Michael S. *Introduction to Operations Research and Management Science: A General Systems Approach.* New York: McGraw-Hill Book Company, 1975.

Rivett, Patrick. *Principles of Model Building.* London: John Wiley and Sons, 1972.

Robichek, Alexander A., and Myers, Stewart L. *Optimal Financing Decisions.* Englewood Cliffs, N.J.: Prentice-Hall, 1965.

Roccaferrera, Guiseppe M. Ferrero di. *Operations Research Models for Business and Industry.* Cincinnati, Ohio: South-Western Publishing Co., 1964.

Roulac, Stephen E. *Modern Real Estate Investment–An Institutional Approach.* San Francisco: Property Press, 1976.

Schlaifer, Robert O. *Analysis of Decisions Under Uncertainty.* New York: McGraw-Hill Book Company, 1969.

Seldin, Maury, and Swesnik, Richard H. *Real Estate Investment Strategy.* New York: Wiley-Interscience, 1970.

Simon, Herbert A. *Administrative Behavior.* 2d ed. New York: Free Press, 1965.

____. *The New Science of Management Decisions.* New York: Harper and Row, 1960.

Singleton, Robert R., and Tyndall, William F. *Games and Programs: Mathematics for Models.* San Francisco: W.H. Freeman and Company, 1974.

Smith, Halbert C.; Tschappat, Carl J.; and Racster, Ronald L. *Real Estate and Urban Development.* Homewood, Ill.: Richard D. Irwin, 1973.

Teichroew, Daniel. *An Introduction to Management Science–Deterministic Models.* New York: John Wiley and Sons, 1964.

Thierauf, Robert J., and Klekamp, Robert C. *Decision Making Through Operations Research.* 2d ed. New York: John Wiley and Sons, 1975.

Tummala, V.M. Rao. *Decision Analysis with Business Applications.* New York: Intext Educational Publications, 1973.

Van Arsdell, Paul M. *Corporation Finance.* New York: Ronald Press Company, 1968.

Van Horne, James C. *Financial Management and Policy.* 3d ed. Englewood Cliffs, N.J.: Prentice-Hall, 1974.

von Neumann, Johan, and Morgenstern, Oscar. *Theory of Games and Ecomonic Behavior.* 2d ed. Princeton, N.J.: Princeton University Press, 1947.

Wagner, Harvey M. *Principles of Management Science.* 2d ed. Englewood Cliffs, N.J.: Prentice-Hall, 1975.

____. *Principles of Operations Research.* 2d ed. Englewood Cliffs, N.J.: Prentice-Hall, 1975.

Wasson, Chester R. *Understanding Quantitative Analysis.* New York: Appleton-Century-Crofts, 1969.

Wendt, Paul F., and Cerf, Alan R. *Real Estate Investment Analysis and Taxation,* New York: McGraw-Hill Book Company, 1969.

White, D.J. *Decision Methodology.* New York: John Wiley and Sons, 1975.

Williams, John Burr. *The Theory of Investment Value.* Cambridge, Mass.: Harvard University Press, 1938.

Wright, M.G. *Discounted Cash Flow.* London: McGraw-Hill Publishing Co., 1967.

Articles

Ackoff, Russell L. "The Development of Operations Research as a Science." *Operations Research* 4 (June 1956): 265-295.

Aldis, Graham. "Management as a Factor in Appraisal." *The Appraisal Journal* 4 (April 1936): 188-193.

Anderson, Robert J., Jr., and Crocker, Thomas D. "Air Pollution and Residential Property Values." *Urban Studies* 8 (October 1971): 171-180.

Aronsohn, Alan J.B. "The Myth of Real Estate as a Tax Shelter." *Real Estate Review* 3 (Summer 1973): 58-65.

Arrow, Kenneth J. "Decision Theory and Operations Research." *Operations Research* 5 (December 1957): 765-774.

Ball, Michael J. "Recent Empirical Work on the Determinants of Relative House Prices." *Urban Studies* 10 (1973): 213-233.

Bacon, Peter W., and Haessler, Robert W. "Simulation and the Capital Asset Pricing Model: A Comment." *Decision Sciences* 6 (January 1975): 202-204.

Baumol, William J. "Economic Models and Mathematics." In *The Structure of Economic Science.* Edited by Sherman Roy Krupp. Englewood Cliffs, N.J.: Prentice-Hall, 1961.

Bedford, E.W. "Why But Real Estate?" *The Appraisal Journal* 13 (April 1945): 135-137.

Bentz, William; Sherr, Lawrence; and Miller, Robert. "Sensitivity Analysis with Interaction Effects." *Decision Sciences* 7 (July 1976): 432-446.

Blazar, Sheldon M., and Hilton, Hugh G. "Investment Opportunities in Existing Apartment Buildings." *Real Estate Review* 6 (Summer 1976): 47-52.

Bleck, Erick K. "Real Estate Investments and Rate of Return." *The Appraisal Journal* 41 (October 1973): 535-547.

Boeckmann, Henry, Jr. "The High Cost of Money and Its Effect on Real Estate Valuations." *The Appraisal Journal* 43 (October 1975): 577-580.

Bower, Richard S., and Lessard, Donald R. "The Problem of the Right Rate: A Comment on Simulation Versus Single-Value Estimates in Capital Expenditure Analysis." *Decision Sciences* 4 (October 1973): 569-571.

Boyce, Byrl N., and Higgins, J. Warren. "Tax Shield Considerations in Real Estate Investment Decisions." *The Real Estate Appraiser* 39 (November/December 1973): 39-44.

Bross, Irwin D.J. "Models." In *Management Systems.* 2d ed. Edited by Peter P. Schoderbek. New York: John Wiley and Sons, 1971.

Bruna, J.A. "Zoning–Its Effect on Property Value." *The Appraisal Journal* 37 (October 1969): 555-561.

Case, Fred. "Comparative Real Estate Investment Experience." *The Appraisal Journal* 28 (July 1960): 337-344.

Clettenberg, Karel J., and Kroncke, Charles O. "How to Calculate Real Estate Return on Investment." *Real Estate Review* 2 (Winter 1973): 105-109.

———. "A Note on Equity Costs in Real Estate Investments." *The Appraisal Journal* 39 (October 1971): 535-539.

Cooper, James R., and Morrison, Cathy A. "Using Computer Simulation to Minimize Risk in Urban Housing Development." *The Real Estate Appraiser* 39 (March/April 1973): 15-26.

Cooper, James R., and Pyhrr, Stephen A. "Forecasting the Rates of Return on an Apartment Investment: A Case Study." *The Appraisal Journal* 41 (July 1973): 312-337.

Crean, Michael J. "Commentary: Monetary and Fiscal Policies: Their Impact on Real Estate." *The Real Estate Appraiser* 42 (March/April 1976), 56-57; also in the *Journal of Property Management* 41 (March/April 1976): 64-65.

Crecine, J.P.; Davis, O.A.; and Jacson, J.E. "Urban Property Markets: Some Empirical Results and Their Implications for Municipal Zoning." *Journal of Law and Economics* 10 (October 1967): 79-99.

Dasso, Jerome J.; Kinnard, William N., Jr.; and Messner, Stephen D. "Lender Participation Financing: Applications of Sensitivity and Investment Analysis." *The Real Estate Appraiser* 37 (July/August 1971): 33–40.

Dawson, Richard E. "Simulation in the Social Sciences." In *Simulation in the Social Sciences: Readings.* Edited by Harold S. Guetzkow. Englewood Cliffs, N.J.: Prentice-Hall, 1962.

Diamond, Arnold H. "Motivations of Investors in Multifamily Housing." *The Real Estate Appraiser* 38 (May/June 1972): 17-24.

Dilmore, Gene. "Internal Rate of Return and the Reinvestment Concept." *The Real Estate Appraiser* 39 (July/August 1973): 29–38.

Downs, Anthony, and Lachman, M. Leanne. "The Current Climate for Real Estate Investment and Development." *Real Estate Review* 4 (Spring 1974): 28–33.

Edwards, Charles E., and Goodwin, Jack S. "An Evaluation of Tax Shields from Declining Balance Depreciation at 1.25 Times the Straight Line Rate." *The Appraisal Journal* 43 (October 1975): 577-580.

Edwards, Ward. "The Theory of Decision Making." *Phychological Bulletin* 51 (July 1954), reprinted as chapter 33 in *Some Theories of Organization.* Edited by Albert H. Rubenstein and Chadwick J. Haverstrob. Homewood, Ill.: Richard D. Irwin, 1960.

Eilon, Samuel, "What Is a Decision?" *Management Science* 16 (December 1969): B172–B189.

Erler, Raymond L. "Rate of Return and Financial Leverage: A Paradigm for Sensitivity Analysis." *The Appraisal Journal* 40 (July 1972): 369-377.

Farrell, Paul B. "Computer-Aided Financial Risk Simulation." *The Appraisal Journal* 37 (January 1969): 58-73.

Feinschreiber, Robert. "A Practical Approach to Rent Roll Analysis." *Real Estate Review* 5 (Summer 1975): 96–100.

Findlay, M. Chapman, III, and Howson, Hugh R., "Optimal Intertemporal Real Estate Ownership, Valuation, and Use." *American Real Estate and Urban Economics Journal* 3 (Summer 1975): 51–66.

Fleisher, Aaron. "The Uses of Simulation." In *Computer Methods in the Analysis of Large-Scale Social Systems.* 2d ed. Edited by James M. Beshers. Cambridge, Mass.: MIT Press. 1968.

Forst, Brian E. "Decision Analysis and Medical Malpractice." *Operations Research* 22 (January/February 1974): 1-12.

Friedman, Harris C. "Real Estate Investment and Portfolio Theory." *Journal of Financial and Quantitative Analysis* (April 1970): 861–874.

Friedman, Jack P. "The Internal Rate of Return Plus the Pull Factor." *The Real Estate Appraiser* 42 (March/April 1976): 29-31.

____. "IRR + Pull Factor v. FMRR: A Reply." *The Real Estate Appraiser* 42 (July/August 1976): 58-60.

Gallagher, Edward F. "Sensitivity Analysis for Apartment House Investment

Property." In *Real Estate Computerization.* Edited by David W. Walters. Berkeley, Calif.: Center for Real Estate and Urban Economics, Research Report no. 35, 1971.

Gau, George W., and Kohlhepp, Daniel B. "Reinvestment Rates and Sensitivity of Rates of Return in Real Estate Investment." *American Real Estate and Urban Economics Journal* 4 (Winter 1976): 69-83.

Gentry, James A. "Simulation Revisited." *Decision Sciences* 4 (October 1973): 572-574.

Gibbons, James E. "Impact of Yields on Value." *The Appraisal Journal* 38 (October 1970): 495-509.

Gibbons, James E., and Rushmore, Stephen. "Using Total Project Analysis to Compete for Investment Capital." *The Appraisal Journal* 43 (October 1975): 491-516.

Glover, Fred. "Managerial Decision and Integer Programming." *The Accounting Review* 44 (April 1969): 300-303.

Godin, Victor B. "The Dollars and Sense of Simulation." *Decision Sciences* 7 (April 1976): 331-342.

Goldie, J. Harry. "Simulation and Irritation." In *Corporate Simulation Models.* Edited by Albert N. Schreiber. Seattle, Wash.: University of Washington Printing Plant, 1970.

Gorry, G. Anthony. "The Development of Managerial Models." *Sloan Management Review* 12 (Winter 1971): 1-15.

Graaskamp, James A. "A Practical Computer Service for the Income Approach." *The Appraisal Journal* 37 (January 1969): 50-57.

Graham, Donald H. Jr. "Owner's Analysis of Yields on Major Real Estate Investments." *The Appraisal Journal* 33 (October 1965): 541-548.

Grayson, C. Jackson, Jr. "The Use of Statistical Techniques in Capital Budgeting." In *Financial Research and Management Decisions.* Edited by Alexander A. Robichek. New York: John Wiley and Sons, 1967.

Grether, D.M., and Mieszkowski, P. "Determinants of Real Estate Values." *Journal of Urban Economics* 1 (April 1974): 127-146.

Hammond, John S. "The Roles of the Manager and Management Scientist in Successful Implementation." *Sloan Management Review* 15 (Winter 1974): 1-24.

Hanford, Lloyd D., Jr. "Expense Ratios and Their Use." *The Appraisal Journal* 41 (January 1973): 100-103.

———. "The Use of Discount Cash Flow Analysis." *The Real Estate Appraiser* 39 (November/December 1973): 31-34.

Harling, John. "Simulation Techniques in Operations Research—A Review." *Operations Research* 6 (May/June 1958): 307-319.

Hawk, Stephen L., and Kroncke, Charles O. "Some Refinements in the Real Estate Investment Decision Process." *The Real Estate Appraiser* 40 (January/February 1974): 13-19.

Hax, Arnoldo C., and Wiig, Karl M. "The Use of Decision Analysis in Capital Investment Problems." *Sloan Management Review* 17 (Winter 1976): 19-48.

Hayes, S.L., and Harlan, L.M. "Real Estate as a Corporate Investment." *Harvard Business Review* 45 (July/August 1967): 144-160.

Hemmer, Edgar H. "How a Computer 'Thinks' About Real Estate." *Real Estate Review* 4 (Winter 1975): 113-123.

Hertz, David B. "Risk Analysis in Capital Investment." *Harvard Business Review* 42 (January/February 1966): 95-106.

Hettenhouse, George W., and Dee, John J. "A Component Analysis of Rates of Return in Real Estate Investment." *American Real Estate and Urban Economics Journal* 4 (Spring 1976): 7-22.

Higgins, J. Warren. "Impact of Federal Taxation on Real Estate Decisions." *The Appraisal Journal* 40 (January 1972): 32-41.

Higgins, Robert C., and Cunningham, R. Hugh. "Computerized Calculations—Rate of Return and Risks in Commercial Property." *The Appraisal Journal* 38 (January 1970): 37-49.

Hitchings, T.C., Jr. "Leverage." *The Real Estate Appraiser* 39 (May/June 1973): 41-45.

Hodges, M.B., Jr. "Computer Progress in Valuation of Income Properties." *The Appraisal Journal* 39 (January 1971): 13-27.

House, William C., Jr. "The Usefulness of Sensitivity Analysis in Capital Investment Decision Making." *Management Accounting* 47 (February 1966): 22-29.

Howard, Ronald A. "The Foundations of Decision Analysis." *IEEE Transactions on Systems Science and Cybernetics* SSC-4 (September 1968): 211-229.

____."Proximal Decision Analysis." *Management Science* 17 (May 1971): 507-541.

Huefner, Ronald J. "Analyzing and Reporting Sensitivity Data." *The Accounting Review* 46 (October 1971): 717-732.

____. "Sensitivity Analysis and Risk Evaluation." *Decision Sciences* 3 (July 1972): 126-135.

Hunter, J.S., and Haylor, Thomas H. "Experimental Designs for Computer Simulation Experiments." *Management Science* 16 (March 1970): 422-434.

Hyman, D.N., and Rasour, E.C., Jr. "Real Property Taxes, Local Public Services, and Residential Property Values." *Southern Economics Journal* 39 (April 1973): 601-611.

Hysom, John, and Juengling, Charles. "Computerized Cash Flow Analysis." *Urban Land* 29 (October 1970): 3-6.

Jansen, Robert E. "Sensitivity Analysis and Integer Linear Programming." *The Accounting Review* 43 (July 1968): 425-446.

Johnson, Glenn L., and Carey Kenneth J. "The Effect of the Investment Credit on Equipment Replacement Decisions." *National Tax Journal* 23 (September 1970): 307-314.

Joy, O. Maurice, and Bradley, Jerry O. "A Note on Sensitivity Analysis of Rates of Return." *Journal of Finance* 31 (March 1976): 63-69.

Kain, J.F., and Quigley, J.M. "Measuring the Value of Housing Quality." *Journal of the American Statistical Association* 65 (June 1970): 532-548.

Landauer, James D. "Real Estate as an Investment." *The Appraisal Journal* 28 October 1960): 426-434.

Lewellen, Wilbur G., and Long, Michael S. "Reply." *Decision Sciences* 4 (October 1973): 575-576.

____. "Simulation Versus Single-Value Estimates in Capital Expenditure Analysis." *Decision Sciences* 3 (October 1972): 19-33.

Little J.D. "Models and Managers: The Concept of a Decision Calculus." *Management Science* 16 (April 1970): B466-B485.

MacCrimmon, Kenneth R. "Description and Normative Implications of the Decision-Theory Postulates." In *Risk and Uncertainty.* Edited by Karl Borck and Jan Mossin. London: Macmillan and Co., 1968.

Maes, Marvin A. "Market Analysis and the Income Approach." *The Appraisal Journal* 44 (October 1976): 577-585.

Maffei, Richard B. "Simulation, Sensitivity and Management Decision Rules." *The Journal of Business* 31 (July 1958): 177-186.

Martin, Wendell H. "Tax Shelter and the Real Estate Analyst." *The Appraisal Journal* 43 (January 1975): 17-28.

McNeeley, W.S. "Money-Making in Real Estate Is a Numbers Game." *Real Estate Review* 2 (Spring 1972): 13-17.

Messner, Stephen D., and Findlay, M. Chapman, III. "Real Estate Investment Analysis: IRR + Pull Factor v. FMRR: A Comment." *The Real Estate Appraiser* 42 (July/August 1976): 58.

____. "Real Estate Investment Analysis: IRR Versus FMRR." *The Real Estate Appraiser* 41 (July/August 1975): 5-20.

Mills, Edwin S. "The Value of Urban Land." In *The Quality of the Urban Environment.* Edited by Harvey S. Perloff. Baltimore, Md.: Johns Hopkins Press, 1969.

Mjosund, Arne. "The Synergy of Operations Research and Computers." *Operations Research* 20 (September/October 1972): 1057-1064.

Montgomery, J. Thomas. "Real Estate Investment Risk—Basic Concepts." *The Appraisal Journal* 44 (January 1976): 9-22.

Muth, Robert F. "The Derived Demand or Urban Residential Land." *Urban Studies* 8 (October 1971): 243-254.

Naylor, Thomas H., and Burdick, Donald S. "The Interface Between Simulation Experiments and Real World Experiments." In *A Survey of Statistical Design and Linear Models.* Edited by Jagdish N. Srivastava. Amsterdam: North-Holland Publishing Co., 1975.

Naylor, Thomas H., and Sasser, W. Earl. "Computer Simulation Experiments with Economic Systems: The Problem of Experimental Design." *Journal of the American Statistical Association* 62 (December 1967): 1315-1337.

———. "The Design of Computer Simulation Experiments." In *The Design of Computer Simulation Experiments.* Edited by Thomas H. Naylor. Durham, N.C.: Duke University Press, 1969.

Nelson, Roland D., and Pollakowski, Arthur J. "The Effect of Financing on Value." *The Appraisal Journal* 40 (April 1972): 279–285.

North, D. Warner. "A Tutorial Introduction to Decision Theory." *IEEE Transactions on Systems Science and Cybernetics* SSC–4 (September 1968): 200-210.

Nourse, M.D. "The Effect of Air Pollution on Housing Values." *Land Economics* 43 (May 1967): 181-189.

Oates, Wallace E. "The Effect of Property Taxes and Local Public Spending on Property Values: An Empirical Study of Tax Capitalization and the Tiebout Hypothesis." *Journal of Political Economy* 77 (November/December 1969): 957-971.

Peatman, John Grey. "The Psychology of Real Estate Investments." *The Appraisal Journal* 10 (October 1942): 335-339.

Pellatt, Peter G.K. "The Analysis of Real Estate Investments Under Uncertainty." *Journal of Finance* 27 (January 1972): 459–471.

Poorvu, William J., and Stevenson, Howard H. "Making the Right Real Estate Bet." *Real Estate Review* 5 (Winter 1976): 61-64.

Pratt, J.W.; Raiffa, Howard; and Schlaifer, Robert O. "The Foundations of Decision Under Uncertainty: An Elementary Exposition." *Journal of the American Statistical Association* 59 (1964): 353-375.

Pyhrr, Stephen A. "Analytical Methods Can Reduce Income Property Loan Losses." *The Real Estate Appraiser* 41 (March/April 1975): 33–43.

———. "A Computer Simulation Model to Measure the Risk in Real Estate Investment." *American Real Estate and Urban Economics Journal* 1 (June 1973): 48–78; also in *The Real Estate Appraiser* 39 (May/June 1973): 13–31.

———. "Real Estate Risk Analysis Goes Scientific." *Real Estate Review* 2 (Fall 1973): 62–67.

Raper, Charles F. "Internal Rate of Return—Handle with Care." *The Appraisal Journal* 44 (July 1976): 405–411.

Rappaport, Alfred. "Integer Programming and Managerial Analysis." *The Accounting Review* 44 (April 1969): 297-299.

———. "Sensitivity Analysis in Decision Making." *The Accounting Review* 42 (July 1967): 441–456.

Ratcliff, Richard U. "Appraisal Is Market Analysis." *The Appraisal Journal* 43 (October 1975): 485–490.

____. "Is There a 'New School of Appraisal Thought?'" *The Appraisal Journal* 40 (October 1972): 522-528.

Ratcliff, Richard U., and Schwab, Bernhard. "Contemporary Decision Theory and Real Estate Investment." *The Appraisal Journal* 38 (April 1970): 165-187.

Recht, J. Richard, and Loewenstein, Louis K. "Variations in Rates of Return." *The Appraisal Journal* 33 (April 1965): 243-248.

Ricks, R. Bruce. "Computers and the Real Estate Investment Process." In *Real Estate Computerization.* Edited by David W. Walters, Berkeley, Calif.: Center for Real Estate and Urban Economics, Research Property no. 35, 1971.

____. "Imputed Equity Returns on Real Estate Financed with Life Insurance Company Loans." *Journal of Finance* 24 (December 1969): 926-937.

Ridker, Ronald G., and Henning, John A. "The Determinants of Residential Property Values with Special Reference to Air Pollution." *Review of Economics and Statistics* 49 (May 1967): 246-257.

Robichek, Alexander A., and Myers, Stewart C. "Note: Conceptual Problems in the Use of Risk-Adjusted Discount Rates." *Journal of Finance* 21 (December 1966): 727-730.

Roulac, Stephen E. "Anatomy of a Land Deal." *Real Estate Review* 4 (Winter 1975): 93-96.

____. "Can Real Estate Returns Outperform Common Stocks?" *Journal of Portfolio Management* 2 (Winter 1976): 26-43.

____. "Life Cycle of a Real Estate Investment." *Real Estate Review* 4 (Fall 1974): 113-117.

____. "The Promoter's Participation Interest as Form of Compensation in Real Estate Syndication." *The Real Estate Appraiser* 39 (May/June 1973): 33-40.

____. "Truth in Real Estate Reporting." *Real Estate Review* 3 (Spring 1973): 90-95.

Rueter, Frederick H. "Externalities in Urban Property Markets: An Empirical Test of the Zoning Ordinance in Pittsburgh." *Journal of Law and Economics* 16 (October 1973): 313-350.

Sabella, E.M. "The Effects of Property Taxes and Local Public Expenditures on the Sales Prices of Residential Dwellings." *The Appraisal Journal* 42 (January 1974): 114-125.

Sarnat, Marshall, and Levy, Haim. "The Relationship of Rules of Thumb to the Internal Rate of Return: A Restatement and Generalization." Journal of Finance 24 (June 1969): 479-490.

Schwab, Bernhard, and Lustig, Peter. "A Comparative Analysis of the Net Present Value and the Benefit-Cost Ratio as Measures of the Economic Desirability of Investments." *Journal of Finance* 24 (June 1969): 507-516.

Seskin, E.P., "Residential Choice and Air Pollution: A General Equilibrium Model." *American Economic Review* 63 (December 1973): 960–967.

Shenkel, William M. "Equity-Capitalization and Investment Decisions: An Application of Conversational Computer Programming." *Journal of Property Management* 34 (March/April 1969a): 76–87.

———. "Cash Flow Analysis: An Application of Conversational Computer Programming." *Journal of Property Management* 34 (July/August 1969b): 165-172.

———. "Cash Flow Analysis and Multiple Regression Techniques: A Computer Application of Apartment Properties." *Journal of Property Management* 34 (November/December 1969c): 264-276.

———. "Net Ground Lease Analysis for Decision Making Purposes." *Journal of Property Management* 35 (March/April 1970): 76–87.

Simon, Herbert A., and Newell, Allen. "Heuristic Problem Solving: The Next Advance in Operations Research." *Operations Research* 6 (January/February 1958): 1-10.

Singer, Bruce. "New Methods of Income Analysis." *The Appraisal Journal* 39 (July 1971): 327-337.

Smith, Halbert C. "Investment Analysis in Appraising." *The Real Estate Appraiser* 33 (September 1967): 19-25.

Smith, Halbert C., and Racster, Ronald L. "Should the Traditional Appraisal Process Be Restructured?" *The Real Estate Appraiser* 36 (November/December 1970): 48-78.

Soelberg, Peer, and Stefaniak, Norbert J. "Impact of the Proposed Tax Reform Bill on Real Estate Investments." *The Appraisal Journal* 38 (April 1970): 188-211.

Soloman, Martin B., Jr. "Uncertainty and Its Effect on Capital Investment Analysis." *Management Science* 12 (April 1966): 334-339.

Spetzler, Carl S. "The Development of a Corporate Risk Policy for Capital Investment Decisions." *IEEE Transactions on Systems Science and Cybernetics* SSC-4 (September 1968): 279-300.

Sprague, Willard F. "Beware the Pro Forma, or, How to Use Sensitivity Analysis." *Real Estate Review* 3 (Summer 1973): 114-116.

Stauss, George. "The Effect of Tax on Yield and Value." *The Appraisal Journal* 37 (July 1969): 386-392.

Stocker, Frederick D. "Effects of Taxation on Urban Land Use." *The Appraisal Journal* 39 (January 1971): 57–69.

Strung, Joseph. "The Internal Rate of Return and the Reinvestment Presumptions." *The Appraisal Journal* 44 (January 1976): 23–33.

Sunley, Emil M., Jr. "Changes in Depreciation and Recapture—Impact on Real Estate Investments." *The Appraisal Journal* 38 (October 1970): 524–535.

Swalm, Ralph O. "A Review of 'Uncertainty and Its Effect on Capital Investment Analysis.'" *The Engineering Economist* 12 (Winter 1967): 123-125.

____. "Utility Theory–Insights into Risk Taking." *Harvard Business Review* 44 (November/December 1966): 123-135.

Teichroew, Daniel; Robicheck, Alexander A.; and Montalbano, Michael. "An Analysis of Criteria for Investment and Financing Decisions Under Certainty." *Management Science* 12 (November 1965): 151-179.

____. "Mathematical Analysis of Rates of Return Under Certainty." *Management Science* 11 (January 1965): 395-403.

Thorne, Oakleigh J. "Real Estate Financial Analysis–The State of the Art." *The Appraisal Journal* 42 (January 1974): 7-37.

Van Horn, Richard L. "Validation of Simulation Results." *Management Science* 17 (January 1971): 247-258.

Walters, David W. "Priorities in Appraisal Analysis." *Assessors Journal* 8 (October 1973a): 3-8.

____. "Just How Important Is Property Management?" *Journal of Property Management* 38 (July/August 1973b): 164-168.

____. "Valuation Sensitivity Analysis." In *Real Estate Computerization.* Edited by David W. Walters. Berkeley, Calif.: Center for Real Estate and Urban Economics, Research Report no. 35, 1971.

Wendt, Paul F. "Cash Flow Analysis by Computer." *Real Estate Review* 2 (Fall 1972): 63-68.

____. "Ellwood, Inwood and IRR." *The Appraisal Journal* 35 (October 1967): 561-574.

____. "Recent Developments in Appraisal Theory." *The Appraisal Journal* 37 (October 1969): 485-500.

Wendt, Paul F., and Tully, Gilbert. "Investment Performance: Common Stocks Versus Apartment Houses." *The Appraisal Journal* 40 (January 1972): 123-127.

Wendt, Paul F., and Wong, Sui N. "Investment Performance: Common Stocks Versus Apartment Houses." *Journal of Finance* 20 (December 1965): 633-646.

Whisler, William D. "Analyzing the Effects of Deviations in Real Estate Investment Analysis." *The Appraisal Journal* 45 (January 1977): 35-48.

____. "Sensitivity Analysis of Rates of Return." *Journal of Finance* 31 (March 1976): 63-69.

White, John R. "How Real Estate Decisions Are Made." *Real Estate Review* 5 (Fall 1975): 42-46.

Wieand, K.F. "Air Pollution and Property Values: A Study of the St. Louis Area." *Journal of Regional Science* 13 (April 1973): 91-95.

Wiese, Robert F. "Investing for True Values." *Barron's.* September 8, 1930.

Wiley, Robert J. "Real Estate Investment Analysis: An Empirical Study." *The Appraisal Journal* 44 (October 1976): 586-592.

Williams, D.R., and Weeks, D.L. "A Technique for Designing and Augmenting Simulation Experiments." *Management Science* 20 (1974): 1389-1392.

Winger, Alan R. "Regional Growth Disparities and the Mortgage Market." *Journal of Finance* 24 (December 1969): 659-662.

Woolsey, R.E.D. "Operations Research and Management Science Today, or, Does an Education in Checkers Really Prepare One for a Life of Chess?" *Operations Research* 20 (May/June 1972): 729-737.

Other Materials

Boyce, Byrl N., ed. *Real Estate Appraisal Terminology.* Cambridge, Mass.: Ballinger Publishing Co., 1975.

Carey, Kenneth, and MacKinnon, Ian. "Sensitivity Analysis of an Equipment Replacement Model." *Proceedings of the Fifth Annual Meeting of the American Institute for Decision Sciences,* November 14-16, 1973, pp. 18-21.

Churchman, C. West. "An Analysis of the Concept of Simulation." In *Symposium on Simulation Models.* Edited by Austin C. Hoggatt and Hederick E. Balderstrom. Cincinnati, Ohio: South-Western Publishing Co., 1963.

Commerce Clearing House. *1977 U.S. Master Tax Guide.* Chicago: Commerce Clearing House, 1977.

Curcio, Richard J., and Gaines, James P. "Intertemporal Investment Revision: The Case of the Purse Real Estate Portfolio." Paper presented at the Financial Management Association Meetings, Montreal, Quebec, October 1976.

———. "The Measurement and Analysis of Risk in Real Estate Investment." Paper presented at the Southern Finance Association Meetings, Atlanta, Ga., November 1976.

Dasso, Jerome. *Computer Applications in Real Estate.* Storrs, Conn.: Center for Real Estate and Urban Economic Studies, Real Estate Report no. 13, 1974.

Davis, Irving F. *A Study of Real Estate Investment Returns to Capital and Management.* Fresno, Calif.: California State University, Bureau of Business Research and Service, Study no. 14, July 1973.

Ellwood, L.W. *Ellwood Tables for Real Estate Appraising and Financing.* Chicago: American Institute of Real Estate Appraisers, 1967.

Federal Reserve Bulletin. Washington, D.C.: Board of Governors of the Federal Reserve System, vols. 52-63, July 1966-March 1976.

Findlay, M. Chapman, III; Messner, Stephen D.; and Tarantello, Rocky A. "An FMRR Simulation Model." Paper presented at Financial Management Association Meetings, Montreal, Quebec, October 1976.

Friedman, Jack P. "The Effect of Three Variables on the Optimal Holding Period for Income-Producing Real Estate." Ph.D. dissertation, Georgia State University, 1975.

Gaumnitz, Jack E. "Analyzing Rates of Return on Real Estate Investments." Lawrence, Kans.: University of Kansas, Working Paper no. 107, 1976.

Gentry, James A. "Linking the Cash Budgeting Process to the Capital Investment Process through Simulation." *1973 AIDS Proceedings* 5 (November 1973): 14-17.

Gross, Jerome S. *Illustrated Encyclopedic Dictionary of Real Estate Terms.* Englewood Cliffs, N.J.: Prentice-Hall, 1969.

Hemmer, Edgar H. "A Valuation Model for Investments in Real Estate." Ph.D. dissertation, Purdue University, 1972.

Higgins, J. Warren. *Impact of Federal Taxation on Real Estate Decisions.* Storrs, Conn.: Center for Real Estate and Urban Economic Studies, Report no. 11, 1971.

Howard, Ronald A. "Decision Analysis: Applied Decision Theory." *Proceedings of the Fourth International Conference on Operational Research,* August 29-September 2, 1966, pp. 55-71.

Institute of Real Estate Management. *Apartment Building Experience Exchange of Rental Income and Operating Expense Data.* Chicago: Institute of Real Estate Management, 1957-62, 1965.

____. *Apartment Building Income-Expense Analysis.* Chicago: Institute of Real Estate Management, 1966-67, 1969-72.

____. *Computer Applications in Property Management Accounting.* Chicago: Institute of Real Estate Management, 1975.

____. *Income-Expense Analysis.* Chicago: Institute of Real Estate Management, 1973-75.

IPFR Publishing Corporation. *Income Property Finance Report.* vol. 1, no. 3. New York: IPFR Publishing Corp., 1977.

____. *Income Property Finance Report.* vol. 1, no. 5. New York: IPFR Publishing Corp., 1977.

Jaffe, Austin J. "Is There a 'New Internal Rate of Return Literature?'" Working Paper, University of Illinois at Urbana-Champaign, 1977.

____. "A Reexamination of the Problem of Management Fee Assessment." Working Paper, University of Illinois at Urbana-Champaign, 1976.

Jaffe, Austin, J., and Sirmans, C.F., Jr. "The Relationship Between Growth Factors, Operating Expense Ratio and Valuation in Real Estate Investment." Working Paper, University of Illinois at Urbana-Champaign, 1977.

Mandel, James, and Morse, Wayne J. "Simulation Versus Single Value Estimates in Capital Expenditure Analysis: A Comment and Analysis." Working Paper, University of Illinois at Urbana-Champaign, 1973.

Miles, Mike, and Pyhrr, Stephen A. "A Framework and Computer Model for

Risk Analysis and Risk Management in Real Property Development." Paper presented at the Financial Management Association Meetings, Montreal, Quebec, October 1976.

National Institute of Farm and Land Brokers. *Federal Taxes Affecting Real Estate.* Rev. ed. with supplement. Chicago: National Institute of Farm and Land Brokers of the National Institute of Real Estate Brokers, 1970.

Naylor, Thomas H. "Computer Simulation: A Managerial Decision Tool." *Papers and Case Histories of the Twenty-Fourth International Systems Meeting,* April 18-21, 1971, series: Ideas for Management, pp. 75-79.

Norton, John H. "The Role of Subjective Probability in Evaluating New Product Ventures." *Chemical Engineering Symposium Series #42, Statistics and Numerical Methods in Chemical Engineering.* New York: American Institute of Chemical Engineers, 1963.

Pyhrr, Stephen, A. "A Proposed Model to Simulate Internal Rate of Return and Risk Characteristics of Investments in Multi-Family Rental Housing." Ph.D. Dissertation, University of Illinois at Urbana-Champaign, 1972.

Pyhrr, Stephen A., and McKinnon, H. Alexander. "Development and Implementation of a Linear Programming Model for Optimally Allocating Real Estate Brokerage Activity." Paper presented at Financial Management Association Meetings, Montreal, Quebec, October 1976.

Rice, T.R. "The Economics of Decision Making." Ph.D. dissertation, Stanford University, 1974.

Ricks, R. Bruce. *Recent Trends in Institutional Real Estate.* Berkeley, Calif.: Center for Real Estate and Urban Economics, Research Report no. 23, 1964.

Smith, Wallace F. *The Low-Rise Speculative Apartment.* Berkeley, Calif.: Center for Real Estate and Urban Economics, Research Report no. 25, 1964.

Teichroew, Daniel. "Computer Simulation—Discussion of the Technique and Comparison of Languages." *Communications of the ACM* 9 (October 1966): 723-741.

Tocher, K.D. "The State of the Art of Simulation—A Survey." *Proceedings of the Fourth International Conference on Operations Research,* August 29-September 2, 1966, pp. 693-701.

U.S. Department of Housing and Urban Development. *Housing and Federal Taxation: Costs and Effectiveness.* June 19, 1973.

——. *Study on Tax Considerations in Multi-Family Housing Investments.* HUD contract H-1227, May 7, 1971.

Walters, David W., ed. *Real Estate Computerization.* Berkeley, Calif.: Center for Real Estate and Urban Economics, Research Report no. 35, 1971.

Wendt, Paul F., and Tandy, Janet. "Evaluation of DCF Models in Real Estate Investment Analysis." Rev. ed., April 1976 (mimeographed).

Wyndelts, Robert W. " Tax Planning and an Analysis of Federal Income Tax Laws: Investment Decisions in Real Estate." Ph.D. dissertation, University of Georgia, 1974.

Yoshimira, Owen K.S., and Cooper, James R. "Real Estate Investment Scanner Simulator (SCANNER)." Computer model, University of Illinois at Urbana-Champaign, 1974.

Appendix

Table A-1
Summary of Another Typical-project Inputs for Testing Data Sensitivity

Variables	*Values*
EGI	\$4103 per month
OE	53.4%
COST	\$20 per square foot
r	10%
REVGR	0% per year
COUP	7.25% per year
L/V	74.2%
TERM	25 years
DEP	straight-line method
TRATE	35%
LIFE	40 years
HP	10 years

Note: All constants are the same as in table 3-1.

Table A-2
***EGI* Sensitivity Functions II, Series I**

Percent	*PV (Dollars)*	*Percent Δ*	*IRR (Percent)*	*Percent Δ*
-50	6,347.09	(89.86)[a]	(2.69)	(127.31)
-40	20,434.86	(67.35)	0.37	(96.24)
-30	34,067.06	(45.57)	3.36	(65.89)
-20	44,248.68	(29.30)	5.63	(42.84)
-10	53,428.06	(14.63)	7.74	(21.42)
0	62,585.12	0.00	9.85	0.00
10	71,742.17	14.63	11.99	21.73
20	80,921.56	29.30	14.16	43.76
30	90,078.61	43.93	16.33	65.79
40	99,235.66	58.56	18.53	88.12
50	108,415.05	73.23	20.74	110.56
60	117,572.10	87.23	22.97	133.20
70	126,729.16	102.49	25.20	155.84
80	135,886.21	117.12	27.46	178.78
90	145,065.59	131.79	29.72	201.73
100	154,222.65	146.42	32.00	224.87

[a]Parentheses indicate negative values.

Table A-3
***OE* Sensitivity Functions II, Series 2**

Percent	*PV (Dollars)*	*Percent Δ*	*IRR (Percent)*	*Percent Δ*
-50	115,099.88	83.91	22.36	127.01
-40	104,667.59	67.24	19.84	101.42
-30	94,048.66	50.27	17.28	75.43
-20	83,626.36	33.62	14.80	50.25
-10	73,007.41	16.65	12.29	24.77
0	62,585.12	0.00	9.85	0.00
10	52,162.83	(16.65)	7.44	(24.47)
20	41,543.89	(33.62)	5.02	(49.04)
30	28,377.51	(54.66)	2.12	(78.48)
40	12,078.01	(80.70)	(1.45)	(114.72)
50	(3,956.24)[a]	(106.32)	(4.91)	(149.85)
60	(19,990.55)	(131.94)	N/A	N/A
70	(36,327.42)	(158.04)	N/A	N/A
80	N/A	N/A	N/A	N/A
90	N/A	N/A	N/A	N/A
100	N/A	N/A	N/A	N/A

[a]Parentheses indicate negative values.

Table A-4
***COST* Sensitivity Functions, II, Series 3**

Percent	*PV (Dollars)*	*Percent Δ*	*IRR (Percent)*	*Percent Δ*
-50	N/A	N/A	20.24	105.48
-40	N/A	N/A	17.40	76.65
-30	N/A	N/A	15.04	52.69
-20	N/A	N/A	13.04	32.39
-10	N/A	N/A	11.33	15.03
0	N/A	N/A	9.85	0.00
10	N/A	N/A	8.56	(13.10)[a]
20	N/A	N/A	7.42	(24.67)
30	N/A	N/A	6.40	(35.03)
40	N/A	N/A	5.50	(44.16)
50	N/A	N/A	4.63	(52.99)
60	N/A	N/A	3.68	(62.64)
70	N/A	N/A	2.70	(72.59)
80	N/A	N/A	1.75	(82.23)
90	N/A	N/A	0.86	(91.27)
100	N/A	N/A	0.06	(99.39)

[a]Parentheses indicate negative values.

Table A-5
***r* Sensitivity Functions II, Series 4**

Percent	*PV (Dollars)*	*Percent Δ*	*IRR (Percent)*	*Percent Δ*
-50	89,747.28	43.40	N/A	N/A
-40	83,246.10	33.01	N/A	N/A
-30	77,336.49	23.57	N/A	N/A
-20	71,957.99	14.98	N/A	N/A
-10	67,056.87	7.15	N/A	N/A
0	62,585.12	0.00	N/A	N/A
10	58,500.26	(6.53)[a]	N/A	N/A
20	54,764.33	(12.50)	N/A	N/A
30	51,343.35	(17.50)	N/A	N/A
40	48,207.14	(22.97)	N/A	N/A
50	45,328.51	(27.57)	N/A	N/A
60	42,683.24	(31.80)	N/A	N/A
70	40,249.51	(35.69)	N/A	N/A
80	38,007.94	(39.27)	N/A	N/A
90	35,940.95	(42.57)	N/A	N/A
100	34,032.81	(45.62)	N/A	N/A

[a]Parentheses indicate negative values.

Table A-6
***REVGR* Sensitivity Functions II, Series 5**

Percent	*PV (Dollars)*	*Percent Δ*	*IRR (Percent)*	*Percent Δ*
-50	N/A	N/A	N/A	N/A
-40	30,256.86	(51.65)[a]	(3.91)	(139.70)
-30	39,702.66	(36.56)	2.38	(75.84)
-20	49,148.47	(21.47)	6.13	(37.77)
-10	56,445.35	(9.81)	8.31	(15.63)
0	62,585.12	0.00	9.85	0.00
10	68,724.89	9.81	11.21	13.81
20	74,864.67	19.62	12.41	25.99
30	81,004.44	29.43	13.50	37.06
40	87,144.21	39.24	14.49	47.11
50	93,283.98	49.05	15.41	56.45
60	99,423.75	58.86	16.26	65.08
70	105,563.53	68.67	17.05	73.10
80	111,703.30	78.48	17.80	80.71
90	117,843.07	88.29	18.50	87.82
100	123,982.84	98.10	19.16	94.52

[a]Parentheses indicate negative values.

Table A-7
***COUP* Sensitivity Functions II, Series 6**

Percent	*PV (Dollars)*	*Percent Δ*	*IRR (Percent)*	*Percent Δ*
-50	84,118.28	34.41	14.62	48.43
-40	80,052.82	27.91	13.76	39.70
-30	75,812.88	21.14	12.84	30.36
-20	71,522.32	14.28	11.90	20.81
-10	67,069.86	7.17	10.89	10.56
0	62,585.12	0.00	9.85	0.00
10	57,951.24	(7.40)	8.77	(10.96)
20	53,302.48	(14.83)	7.65	(22.34)
30	48,516.86	(22.48)	6.49	(34.11)
40	43,732.25	(30.12)	5.30	(46.19)
50	38,127.15	(39.08)	3.92	(60.20)
60	30,999.84	(50.47)	2.18	(77.87)
70	23,113.45	(63.07)	0.19	(98.07)
80	15,254.16	(75.63)	(1.82)	(118.48)
90	7,244.47	(88.42)	(3.91)	(139.70)
100	(690.64)[a]	(101.10)	(6.01)	(161.02)

[a]Parentheses indicate negative values.

Table A-8
***L/V* Sensitivity Functions II, Series 7**

Percent	*PV (Dollars)*	*Percent Δ*	*IRR (Percent)*	*Percent Δ*
-50	125,959.76	101.26	7.05	(28.43)
-40	113,318.99	81.06	7.34	(25.48)
-30	100,678.23	60.87	7.70	(21.83)
-20	87,866.65	40.40	8.19	(16.85)
-10	75,225.91	20.20	8.86	(10.05)
0	62,585.12	0.00	9.85	0.00
10	49,944.37	(20.20)[a]	11.50	16.74
20	37,303.61	(40.40)	14.82	50.46
30	24,492.02	(60.87)	26.74	171.47
40	N/A	N/A	N/A	N/A

[a]Parentheses indicate negative values.

Table A-9
***TERM* Sensitivity Functions II, Series 8**

Percent	*PV (Dollars)*	*Percent Δ*	*IRR (Percent)*	*Percent Δ*
-50	52,938.25	(15.41)[a]	8.29	(15.84)
-40	56,313.80	(10.62)	8.72	(11.47)
-30	58,653.54	(6.28)	9.09	(7.72)
-20	60,348.25	(3.57)	9.39	(4.67)
-10	61,615.26	(1.55)	9.64	(2.13)
0	62,585.12	0.00	9.85	0.00
10	63,341.02	1.21	10.02	1.73
20	63,938.47	2.16	10.18	3.35
30	64,415.92	2.93	10.30	4.57
40	64,800.86	3.54	10.41	5.69
50	65,113.45	4.04	10.49	6.50
60	65,368.70	4.45	10.56	7.21
70	65,578.18	4.78	10.62	7.82
80	65,750.72	5.06	10.67	8.32
90	65,893.30	5.29	10.72	8.83
100	66,011.42	5.47	10.75	9.14

[a]Parentheses indicate negative values.

Table A-10
***DEP* Sensitivity Functions II, Series 9**

Percent	*PV (Dollars)*	*Percent Δ*	*IRR (Percent)*	*Percent Δ*
0	62,585.12	0.00	9.85	0.00
25	63,488.24	1.44	10.04	1.93
50	64,970.53	3.81	10.41	5.69
100	67,741.45	8.24	11.08	12.49

Table A-11
***TRATE* Sensitivity Functions II, Series 10**

Percent	*PV (Dollars)*	*Percent Δ*	*IRR (Percent)*	*Percent Δ*
-50	69,702.70	11.37	11.51	16.85
-40	68,279.19	9.10	11.18	13.50
-30	66,855.67	6.82	10.85	10.15
-20	65,432.16	4.55	10.52	6.80
-10	64,008.63	2.27	10.19	3.45
0	62,585.12	0.00	9.85	0.00
10	61,161.61	(2.27)[a]	9.52	(3.35)
20	59,738.10	(4.55)	9.19	(6.70)
30	58,314.57	(6.82)	8.86	(10.05)
40	56,891.06	(9.10)	8.53	(13.40)
50	55,467.54	(11.37)	8.20	(16.75)
60	54,044.04	(13.65)	7.87	(20.10)
70	52,620.51	(15.92)	7.53	(23.55)
80	51,196.99	(18.20)	7.20	(26.90)
90	49,773.48	(20.47)	6.87	(30.25)
100	48,349.96	(22.75)	6.54	(33.60)

[a]Parentheses indicate negative values.

Table A-12
***LIFE* Sensitivity Functions II, Series 11**

Percent	*PV (Dollars)*	*Percent Δ*	*IRR (Percent)*	*Percent Δ*
-50	65,823.97	5.18	10.65	8.12
-40	64,744.36	3.45	10.37	5.28
-30	63,973.20	2.22	10.18	3.35
-20	63,394.83	1.29	10.03	1.83
-10	62,945.00	0.58	9.96	1.12
0	62,585.12	0.00	9.85	0.00
10	62,290.69	(0.47)[a]	9.79	(0.61)
20	62,045.32	(0.86)	9.73	(1.22)
30	61,837.70	(1.19)	9.69	(1.62)
40	61,659.74	(1.48)	9.65	(2.03)
50	61,505.51	(1.73)	9.61	(2.44)
60	61,370.55	(1.74)	9.58	(2.74)
70	61,251.49	(2.13)	9.56	(2.94)
80	61,145.64	(2.30)	9.53	(3.25)
90	61,050.94	(2.45)	9.51	(3.45)
100	60,965.70	(2.59)	9.49	(3.65)

[a]Parentheses indicate negative values.

Table A-13
***HP* Sensitivity Functions II, Series 12**

Percent	*PV (Dollars)*	*Percent Δ*	*IRR (Percent)*	*Percent Δ*
-50	63,100.57	0.98	10.00	1.52
-40	63,136.18	0.88	9.98	1.32
-30	63,043.46	0.73	9.97	1.22
-20	62,921.07	0.54	9.92	0.71
-10	62,768.41	0.29	9.89	0.41
0	62,585.12	0.00	9.85	0.00
10	62,371.70	(0.34)[a]	9.82	(0.30)
20	62,128.68	(0.73)	9.78	(0.71)
30	61,856.97	(1.16)	9.74	(1.12)
40	61,557.86	(1.64)	9.69	(1.62)
50	61,232.65	(2.16)	9.65	(2.03)
60	60,882.76	(2.72)	9.60	(2.54)
70	60,509.86	(3.32)	9.56	(2.94)
80	60,115.44	(3.95)	9.51	(3.45)
90	59,701.21	(4.61)	9.46	(3.96)
100	59,268.94	(5.30)	9.41	(4.47)

[a]Parentheses indicate negative values.

Table A-14
Summary of Present Value Percentage Changes for Twelve Variables

Percent	*EGI*	*OE*	*COST*	*r*	*REVGR*	*COUP*	*L/V*	*TERM*	*DEP*	*TRATE*	*LIFE*	*HP*
-50	(89.86)[a]	83.91	–	43.40	N/A	34.41	101.26	(15.41)	–	11.37	5.18	0.98
-40	(67.35)	67.24	–	33.01	(51.65)	27.91	81.06	(10.62)	–	9.10	3.45	0.88
-30	(45.57)	50.27	–	23.57	(36.56)	21.14	60.87	(6.28)	–	6.82	2.22	0.73
-20	(29.30)	33.62	–	14.98	(21.47)	14.28	40.40	(3.57)	–	4.55	1.29	0.54
-10	(14.63)	16.65	–	7.15	(9.81)	7.17	20.20	(1.55)	–	2.27	0.58	0.29
0	0.00	0.00	–	0.00	0.00	0.00	0.00	0.00	0.00	0.00	0.00	0.00
10	14.63	(16.65)	–	(6.53)	9.81	(7.40)	(20.20)	1.21	–	(2.27)	(0.47)	(0.34)
20	29.30	(33.62)	–	(12.50)	19.62	(14.83)	(40.40)	2.16	–	(4.55)	(0.86)	(0.73)
30	43.93	(54.66)	–	(17.96)	29.43	(22.48)	(60.87)	2.93	1.44	(6.82)	(1.19)	(1.16)
40	58.56	(80.70)	–	(22.97)	39.24	(30.12)	N/A	3.54	–	(9.10)	(1.48)	(1.64)
50	73.23	(106.32)	–	(27.57)	49.05	(39.08)	–	4.04	3.81	(11.37)	(1.73)	(2.16)
60	87.86	(131.94)	–	(31.80)	58.86	(50.47)	–	4.45	–	(13.65)	(1.94)	(2.72)
70	102.49	(158.04)	–	(35.69)	68.67	(63.07)	–	4.78	–	(15.92)	(2.13)	(3.32)
80	117.12	N/A	–	(39.69)	78.48	(75.63)	–	5.06	–	(18.20)	(2.30)	(3.95)
90	131.79	N/A	–	(42.57)	88.29	(88.42)	–	5.29	–	(20.47)	(2.45)	(4.61)
100	146.42	N/A	–	(45.62)	98.10	(101.10)	–	5.47	8.24	(22.75)	(2.59)	(5.30)

[a]Parentheses indicate negative values.

Table A-15
Summary of Internal Rate of Return Percentage Changes for Twelve Variables

Percent	*EGI*	*OE*	*COST*	*r*	*REVGR*	*COUP*	*L/V*	*TERM*	*DEP*	*TRATE*	*LIFE*	*HP*
-50	(127.31)[a]	127.01	105.48	–	N/A	48.43	(28.43)	(15.84)	–	16.85	8.12	1.52
-40	(96.24)	101.42	76.65	–	(139.30)	39.70	(25.48)	(11.47)	–	13.50	5.28	1.32
-30	(65.89)	75.43	52.69	–	(75.84)	30.36	(21.83)	(7.72)	–	10.15	3.35	1.22
-20	(42.84)	50.25	32.39	–	(37.77)	20.81	(16.85)	(4.67)	–	6.80	1.83	0.71
-10	(21.42)	24.77	15.03	–	(15.63)	10.56	(10.05)	(2.13)	–	3.45	1.12	0.41
0	0.00	0.00	0.00	–	0.00	0.00	0.00	0.00	0.00	0.00	0.00	0.00
10	21.73	(24.47	(13.10)	–	13.81	(10.96)	16.75	1.75	–	(3.35)	(0.61)	(0.30)
20	43.76	(49.04)	(24.67)	–	25.99	(22.34)	50.46	3.35	–	(6.70)	(1.22)	(0.71)
30	65.79	(78.48)	(35.03)	–	37.06	(34.11)	171.47	4.57	1.93	(10.05)	(1.62)	(1.12)
40	88.12	(114.72)	(44.16)	–	47.11	(46.19)	N/A	5.67	–	(13.40)	(2.03)	(1.62)
50	110.56	(149.85)	(52.99)	–	56.45	(60.20)	–	6.50	5.69	(16.75)	(2.44)	(2.03)
60	133.20	N/A	(62.64)	–	65.08	(77.87)	–	7.21	–	(20.10)	(2.74)	(2.54)
70	155.84	N/A	(72.59)	–	73.10	(98.07)	–	7.82	–	(23.55)	(2.94)	(2.94)
80	178.78	N/A	(82.23)	–	80.71	(118.48)	–	8.32	–	(26.90)	(3.25)	(3.45)
90	201.73	N/A	(91.27)	–	87.82	(139.70)	–	8.83	–	(30.25)	(3.45)	(3.96)
100	224.87	N/A	(99.39)	–	94.52	(161.02)	–	9.14	12.49	(33.60)	(3.65)	(4.47)

[a]Parentheses indicate negative values.

Author Index

Subject Index

About the Author

Austin J. Jaffe is currently assistant professor of finance and real estate in the Department of Finance at the University of Oregon. He received the B.S. degree in finance with highest honors in 1974, the M.S. degree in finance in 1975, and the Ph.D. degree in finance in 1978 from the University of Illinois at Urbana-Champaign.

Dr. Jaffe has also worked as a property manager and adviser for a number of firms during the past few years. Currently, he is involved in the development of real estate education in the State of Oregon. He is an active member of Beta Gamma Sigma and Rho Epsilon, the honorary real estate fraternity. He also holds membership in several professional organizations, including American Real Estate and Urban Economics Association, American Finance Association, Western Finance Association, and Financial Management Association.

He has recently contributed articles dealing with real estate investment analysis and professional property management to the *American Real Estate and Urban Economics Journal, The Appraisal Journal, The Real Estate Appraiser, Journal of Property Management, Real Estate Review, Real Estate Issues,* and others.